# A Craving for Crab

## CHRISTINE QUINN
illustrated by *JENNIFER BELLINGER*

ISLAND PUBLISHING

Cover and Illustrations: Jennifer Bellinger- Except 5 easy steps to clean crab and crab pots.
Editing: A. Heidi Wrightsman
Layout and Design: Dallas Drotz and Printery Communications
Indexing: Beth Nauman-Montana   www.salmonbayindexing.com

Library of Congress Control Number : 2004093944
Library of Congress Cataloging- in – publication
A craving for crab / Christine Quinn; illustrated by Jennifer Bellinger.
p. cm.
Includes bibliographical references and index.
LCCN 2004093944
ISBN 0-9755929-0-4
1. Cookery (Crabs)    I. Bellinger, Jennifer.
II. Title.
TX754.C83Q56 2004            641.6'95
                            QBI04-700433


A Craving for Crab is produced and printed in the U.S.A.

Island Publishing
15652 Point Monroe Drive NE
Bainbridge Island, WA 98110

## Dedication

My Husband, The love of my life who makes it all possible.
Who without, this book and my wonderful life would not exist. Who
shared his love of crab and crabbing with me.

My family and my wonderful children Josh and Lindsey.

## Acknowledements

Debi Bozanich for your perseverance in painstakingly checking and re-
checking each and every recipe. Your help was invaluable.

Jennifer Bellinger for the gorgeous cover and graphics.

Thanks to Kelly Macdonald, a fabulous cook, for sharing your Special
Sauce and Corn Salsa Recipes and most of all your Crab Stuffed
Roasted Poblanos. One of the best meals I've ever had.

Mea Gram for your editing expertise.

"I would trade a whole catch
of lobsters for a good Dungeness crab."
*-James Beard*

"Holding a glass of wine in the right hand,
grasping a crab claw in the left hand,
and drifting along in a boat filled with wine,
ah, my life is totally satisfied!"
*-Anonymous Chinese poem dated 256-420 A.D.*

# *CONTENTS*

## CHAPTER 3- SOUPS, CHOWDERS & BISQUE

## CHAPTER 4- MAIN DISHES & ENTRÉES

## CHAPTER 5 – PERFECT ACCOMPANIMENTS & THE PERFECT ENDING

# CHAPTER 6- SAUCES, SALSAS, & FLAVORED BUTTERS   page 119

# CHAPTER 7- CRAB CULTURE

# CHAPTER 8- SOURCES AND RESOURCES

# introduction
# & crab primer

# INTRODUCTION

I live on the Olympic Peninsula in Washington State. My husband and I are fortunate that Dungeness crab is plentiful here. We take our small boat out and set out crab pots, which are basically large cages with a small box inside containing bait. Bait consists of fish scraps, chicken parts, clams and whatever we can come up with. We have an ongoing debate about which bait works best. I'm for fish heads, while my husband thinks it is chicken parts that bring them in. We have a friend who one day, unable to find anything else, used boneless, skinless chicken breasts and though expensive, it worked quite well. So well in fact, he beat us that day.

Only male Dungeness may be kept; we throw back any females. We also throw back any under 6¼ inches (the minimum legal size) and any soft-shells. There is a limit in the state of Washington of six crabs per person, per day. We often catch or exceed our limit, in which case we throw back the extras. Several times we have found ourselves with empty traps and all the bait gone. This was a mystery to us until one day looking out the window my husband happened to see someone pulling up one of our four pots. We got the boat's registration number and called the Fish and Game Department. The culprits admitted to the theft (kind of) and were issued a citation with a hefty fine. Since that incident four years ago, we've caught several other rustlers. Sometimes it is the person you would least suspect. One person we caught had at the start of the season placed his pots in front of our house, and asked us to keep an eye on them, along with our own. We have even had our crab stolen and the pots re-baited. In fact, watching out our front window for crab rustlers has become a favorite pastime of our guests. One year, my nephew Austin spotted a rustler and yelled to my husband who verified that the guy was indeed pulling up one of our pots. My husband was there to meet him when he arrived at the dock!

Once we get home with our catch my husband cooks the crab outside in a propane cooker with a 10-gallon pot (also known as a deep-fat turkey fryer). He adds salt and white vinegar to the water. A day's limit of 12 crabs often has our crab cooker virtually overflowing with crab.

This cookbook came about as a result of "The Crab Cracker". Let me explain: my husband's grandfather invented a device to crack crab. It is basically a wooden board with a handle that comes down and cracks the crab. One night we had friends over for dinner who marveled at the ease and speed with which "The Crab Cracker" cracked our crab and they were even more impressed with the quality of the cracked crab, i.e. no shells embedded in the crab. I initiated a search for crab crackers and quickly found that nut crackers masquerading as crab crackers were it! My husband made several changes to his grandfather's design and we were in business. (Well - it hasn't been quite that simple!) At that time, I thought it would be great to include a small booklet with crab recipes to accompany "The Crab Cracker." Well, the little booklet turned into a full-fledged cookbook, over three years in the making. I've had a lifelong passion for food, cooking and, of course, crab. I've always loved crab. I can honestly say I never tire of eating crab. Friends are often surprised when dining out that I order crab.

How fortunate we are to enjoy crab anytime anyplace. Thanks to improved transportation and shipping methods, crab is no longer just a regional indulgence. With crab available in markets and restaurants in all parts of the country, a simple phone call can result in fresh crab at your doorstep literally within hours. Crab cooking and eating can create a festive mood. These recipes and this book can be the beginning of your adventures with this tasty, delectable crustacean. I hope that they inspire and prompt you to make them your own. Indulge yourself: have fun, be creative and improvise when the mood strikes you; and most of all, enjoy !

## CRAB PRIMER

Crab types vary around the coasts of the United States. Although different types of crab are often interchangeable in recipes, I've discovered a definite bias concerning crab depending on where the person in question hails from. I've also found that same bias with chefs and in cookbooks. Invariably, I've found when reading a cookbook or article on crab, depending on what region the author is from, there is a decided preference on crab of that region, often proclaiming that to be the best. I'd say that the East coast - West coast rivalry is alive and well. But it's about the crab. In fact, during a convention of mayors, an argument arose about who cooked crab better, people on the East or West coasts. As a result, crab cooking contests were held on both coasts resulting in a final cook-off in San Francisco. The West coast won. Ray Marshall of Acapulco Restaurant, with his crab enchiladas, developed the winning recipe. As for me, I share none of those biases. I love crab of all types.

Crab is extremely versatile; it can be enjoyed as plain or as dressed up fancy as you like. Crab lends itself well to a variety of preparations and cuisines and it's simply exquisite served in the shell. And best of all crab is good for you, coming in at 110 calories and just 1.2 grams of fat per 3.5 ounce serving, and it only gets better. Crab is an excellent source of chromium, which helps to raise the levels of HDL (good cholesterol). Crab also contains goodly amounts of selenium, a trace element that works as an antioxidant, detoxifying carcinogenic substances. And more good news, eating Dungeness crab is politically correct. In fact, it is on the "recommended list" of organizations such as the National Resources Defense Council and many other marine protection groups.

## TYPES OF CRAB

### Blue Crab
*Callinectes Sapidus*
Blue crab is the toast of the East and Gulf coasts. The blue crab's name Callinectes Sapidus means beautiful swimmer savory. The blue crab is particularly abundant in Chesapeake Bay whose name has become synonymous with crab cuisine. Louisiana has also staked its claim to crab cuisine with its Cajun and Creole influences. South Carolina's Charleston She Crab Soup is a delicacy par excellence. Blue crab is the only crab available in hard and soft shell form. Blue crab meat is available year-round in the pasteurized form, live crabs are seasonal and much more plentiful during the warm water months of the year.  Fresh or pasteurized cooked crabmeat is usually available for purchase as lump, flake, or claw meat

In order to grow, a blue crab must shed its shell. The crab actually grows a new shell underneath its old shell and then breaks out of the old shell. It emerges from its old shell with a paper-thin soft shell that will harden in a few days. The shedding process is repeated up to 25 times during a crab's lifetime. While the females are in their molted state, the male blue crab will protect her. The female however shows no such mercy and will devour any male that comes her way.

*Soft-shell crab* has exquisite flavor because it has fattened up to make it through until it is hard enough to scavenge for food again. When in the soft shell state, the entire crab is edible and fabulously delicious. Soft-Shells are sold live and frozen. They may be deep-fried, sautéed, or grilled, though I must profess a preference for fried.

*Hard shell crab* have a sweet delicate flavor and can be served hot or cold and lends itself to a wide variety of preparation methods. Fifteen per cent of the weight of a blue crab is meat.

### Dungeness Crab
*Cancer Magister*
The favorite of the West coast!  Often associated with Fisherman's Wharf in San Francisco, the name Dungeness comes from the town of the same name on Washington's Olympic Peninsula. Dungeness crab is available year round. It is harvested in California during the winter. Near San Francisco the season begins November 15th (cracked crab is as much a tradition at some tables as turkey). The Oregon and Washington crabbing season lasts longer into spring, while in British Columbia the peak season starts in April and the Alaska Dungeness fishery occurs mainly in summer.

Only males may be kept. The females are returned to reproduce.

Fortunately the hefty size of Dungeness, up to four pounds and averaging 1 ½ to 3 pounds, means there is a lot of meat. In fact, 25 per cent of the weight of a Dungeness crab is meat and can easily be retrieved.

Succulent Dungeness has a distinctive buttery sweet flavor and tender white meat in the body. According to Mark Bittman in his book *Fish: The Complete Guide to Buying and Cooking,* "this great-tasting Pacific crab is better compared to Maine lobster than to blue crab; it's that good and that meaty." Steamed or boiled, served with sourdough bread and a simple green salad is an all time favorite. Dungeness crab combines well with a myriad of seasonings and sauces and lends itself to all preparations.

## King Crab
*Cancer Paralithodos*
Paralithodos literally means the king. These delicious giants can weigh up to 25 pounds with a six-foot leg span. There are three species of king: red, rlue and brown, with the red being the most abundant and preferred. Elegant king crab is prized for its delicate sweet flavor and wonderful texture. The meat is snowy white and edged with a beautiful red. Most king crab goes to what is referred to in the industry as "white table cloth restaurants". King crab is generally sold frozen; it is usually cooked and flash frozen on the boat. King crab freezes exceptionally well. The secret to retaining all the flavor and texture is a slow thaw (1 or 2 days) in the refrigerator. King crab is most commonly served broiled with butter, my favorite way to enjoy king crab.

## Peekytoe Crab
*Cancer Irroratus*
Peekytoe crab is also known as Maine crab, sand crab, and rock crab.  The peekytoe, once a throw away by-product of lobster fishing, has become the darling of the culinary world. Sought after by some of the most discriminating chefs; Thomas Keller of French Laundry, Daniel Bould of Restaurant Daniel and Wolfgang Puck of Spago just to name a few. How did this happen you may ask? In 1997, Rob Mitchell, a seafood wholesaler in Portland, Maine, re-named the crab peekytoe from the slang name Picked Toe used by the Maine locals to describe the peculiar inwardly turning sharp points of the crab's legs. "Picked" is Maine slang for pointed. The Maine accent contributed to the resulting name. What sets the crab apart is the care with which it is handled. A cottage industry has sprung up around this crab. Peekytoe is extremely perishable and cannot be shipped live. Lobstermen's wives do much of the picking (separation of meat from shell). Until recently, they prepared the crab in their home kitchens, but due to new federal safety regulations, the crab is now prepared in structures built next to their homes. Peekytoe weigh less than one pound. The sweet, delicately flavored meat goes well with a variety of flavors and cooking styles.

## Stone Crab

*Cancer Quanbumi (menippe mercenaria)*

Florida lays claim to this delicious delicacy. The stone crab's claws are the only part that is eaten. A stone crab's claws make up more than half of its body weight. Fishermen twist off one claw and return the crab to the sea, where the crab will regenerate its claw within 18 months. During the life of a stone crab, the same claw may be regenerated three or four times. Females with eggs are returned intact. The law requires these claws to be boiled or steamed for 7 minutes and then either put on ice or frozen; this prevents the meat from sticking to the shells. The fishing season for stone crab is October 15th to May 15th. Stone crab is available year–round because the majority of the claws taken are frozen. Stone crab has a firm texture and a sweet succulent flavor. Stone crab can be served warm or cold with a sauce (mustard being the most popular) or the meat its self works wonderfully in recipes.

## Snow Crab

*Cancer Quanbumi (chinoecetes opilio)*

If you've eaten at a seafood buffet, you are familiar with snow crab. Snow crab is actually several species including tanner, spider and queen crab. Snow crab takes its name from their snow-white colored meat. These three species got their shared name because they have a similar taste and have snow-white colored meat. Snow crab is mainly harvested in Alaska, thus it is generally sold frozen. Snow crab typically weighs between 1½ and 3 pounds. Although snow crabmeat is quite good, the crab's legs are thin and the meat can be difficult to get out. Snow crab legs may be sold as already split. Like king crab, snow crab is best with a slow thaw in the refrigerator. Snow crab is also versatile and lends itself to all preparations.

## PURCHASING CRAB

When possible, it is best to purchase live crab. Taking it home and cooking it can be a real adventure. Nothing surpasses the flavor of steaming crab, fresh out of the pot. Now, if you are serving chilled crab or are picking the meat out for a recipe, then you may wish to purchase crab that has already been cooked. The exceptions would be: stone crab claws, king and snow crab, which are almost always frozen.

### Buying Live Dungeness Crab

Look for lively active crabs. Lethargic ones can taste bitter due to digestive juices permeating the meat and never, never buy a dead crab. Once a crab dies, it begins to spoil rapidly and harmful bacteria will quickly form. Once you select your crab, have your fishmonger cook and clean it for you or bring it home alive. Look for dark color, Dungeness crab in its prime is dark brown to purplish and if it has barnacles all the better. That means it has been in its shell for a while and fattening up. Also make sure that if the crab is coming from a tank, the fishmonger lets the crab drain before weighing it. Crab is expensive enough without paying for water.

When purchasing live crabs, it's always best to buy them near to the time you will be cooking them. Live crabs will keep a day maybe two in the refrigerator, but after about 12 hours mortality rates rise. Also, the cold temperature of the refrigerator renders them inactive making cooking and cleaning easier. Keep live crabs loosely covered with a moist towel or paper. If a crab in the refrigerator does perish, cook as soon as possible.

*The claw tips (pointed tips of the leg) from the crab make nifty crab pickers.*

### Whole Cooked Dungeness Crab

When buying whole cooked crab, look for crab that feels heavy in its shell. It should be a brilliant red and again, barnacles are a good indicator of a meaty crab. Look for legs that are tightly drawn, splayed legs indicate the crab was dead when cooked. Avoid any crab with a fishy or ammonia odor. Crab should have a fresh salt-water aroma. Find out when the crab was cooked. Crab should be consumed within three to four days of being cooked and until then, kept refrigerated.

## CLEANING CRAB

If cleaning a crab seems daunting don't worry, it won't after your first one. The time-honored tradition of cleaning crab is to first cook them by plunging them alive into boiling water, and cleaning the crab after cooking. This is a topic of debate between my husband and myself. In my opinion, it is best to clean the crab prior to cooking. There are several reasons for this: live cleaning maintains the freshest tasting crabmeat, cleaning prior to cooking eliminates the visceral taste that crab can sometimes take on, there's virtually no odor during cooking, cleaned crab take up less space in the cooking pot, and in many preparations such as grilling and stir-frying, soups and stews the crab is not cooked twice. Cleaned crab cools much faster after cooking and lastly and most importantly, the crab is ready to eat! My husband prefers cleaning the crab after cooking because… that's the way he's always done it.

## 5 Easy Steps to Cleaning Crab

1.    Hold crab with one hand, place thumb under shell at midpoint and pull off carapace (shell) (Rinse and save if using for presentation)

2.    Under cold running water turn crab over and remove the gills using a spoon edge or your fingers.

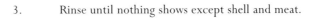

3.    Rinse until nothing shows except shell and meat.

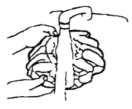

4.    Break crab in half along the center line, creating two "sections" with legs/claws attached.

5.    Remove the legs and claws. Now the crab is ready for cracking!

*Bon Appetit !*

## BASIC COOKING METHODS

### Three Methods for Cleaning Crab prior to Cooking are:

*Boiling*

Boil the crab for one minute. Remove the crab from the pot, rinse with cold water and proceed with cleaning. Once done cleaning, proceed with preparation.

*Live-backing*

Refrigerate crab or place in ice water for about 10 minutes; this renders the crab docile. Holding the crab body pull off the carapace (top shell) with one quick rip. This action kills the crab instantly, but be careful of the pincers, which can catch you with reflex action. Proceed with cleaning.

*Mallet and Knife*

Refrigerate the crab or place it in ice water for about 10 minutes, to render the crab docile Place a large heavy knife over the center of the belly lengthwise and rap sharply with a mallet to cut through, using one quick motion, chopping the crab in half .This method also kills the crab instantly. Proceed with cleaning. (Use one of the methods above if you will be using the upper shell for presentation).

> *NEVER CROSS-CONTAMINATE. Always keep uncooked and cooked crab from coming in contact with each other.Sanitize work space between preparations.*

### Basic Methods of Cooking Dungeness Crab

*Boiling*

Bring a large pot of salted water to a rolling boil. Drop the crab into the boiling water. When water return to a full boil, begin timing 15- 20 minutes for whole crab (uncleaned). Cook cleaned crab 12 minutes. If not serving immediately, place crab in cold water or ice.

*Steaming*

Use a steamer if you have one, if not, any big pot will do as long as you have something to put in the bottom that raises the crabs out of the water while steaming, a rack or a colander placed upside down works well. Add 2-4 inches of water to the pot. Bring the water to a full boil and add crab. Cover the pot tightly and steam 20-25 minutes (7-10 minutes if re-heating) until the shells are bright red. Once cooked, carefully remove the crabs with a pair of tongs. If not serving immediately, place crab in cold water or ice.

*Note*

If you are cooking a large quantity of crabs an outdoor propane cooker (also known as a turkey deep-fryer) is ideal. The cookers come with a basket, making for easy removal.

## Buying Live Blue Crab

Live blue crabs are frequently sold by the dozen or by the bushel and half bushel; a bushel contains approximately six dozen crabs. The actual number of crabs in a bushel can vary depending on the size of the crab.

Male hard crabs are called "Jimmies" and mature female crabs are usually called "Sooks". Jimmies are generally larger and meatier, therefore more desirable for eating whole, though don't think a big crab is always the best crab; the heaviest crab often come in small shells. Pass on crab that have recently molted as they will be light, hollow (full of water), and won't contain much meat. A recently molted crab will have a top shell with a grayish cast and a lustrous white abdomen. Crabs nearing the end of their molt cycle will be heavy and full of meat. Always ask for "fat" or "heavy" crabs.

### Blue Crab Grading (sizes)

| | |
|---|---|
| Colossal | 6 ½ inches or more. |
| Jumbo | 6 to 6 ½ inches in size. |
| Large | 5 ½ to 6 inches in size. |
| Medium | 5 to 5 ½ inches in size. |
| Small | 4 ½ to 5 inches in size, usually females. |

## Basic Method of Cooking Blue Crab

### Boiling

Bring a large pot of salted water to a rolling boil. Drop the crab into the boiling water. Cover and return to the boiling point. Reduce heat; simmer for 12-15 minutes. For crabs cleaned prior to cooking, reduce cooking time by 5-7 minutes. The crab may be boiled in seasoned water by using a commercially packaged blend of spices designed for boiling crab such as Zatarain's Crab Boil. If not serving immediately, place crab in cold water or ice.

### Steaming

Use a steamer if you have one, if not, any big pot will do as long as you have something to put in the bottom that raises the crabs out of the water while steaming, a rack or a colander placed upside down work well. Add about 2-4 inches of water to the pot. Bring the water to a full boil and add crab (if desired sprinkle each layer of crabs with Old Bay or other seasoning.) Cover the pot tightly and steam 20-25 minutes, until the shells are bright orange. Once cooked, carefully remove the crabs with a pair of tongs. If not serving immediately, place crab in cold water or ice.

Before steaming or boiling crabs, you may "chill" them in the refrigerator; the cold temperature renders them inactive and easier to place in the pot.

## Buying Soft-Shell Crab

Soft-shell crab is shipped live but typically marketed as fresh. Once a crab molts, it is extremely weak and often will appear dead. In many cases, the soft-shell crab will move when touched. The only real indicator to determine the freshness of the soft-shell is the smell. If there is a distinct ammonia odor do not purchase. Soft-shells that have perished, but have no odor, are still fresh enough to eat.

Soft-shells may be sold in individually or in trays. The number of soft-shells per tray varies by size, a tray of primes would contain 4 dozen soft-shells. Choose crabs with soft moist shells; the new gray shells beginning to form should appear tender, not mushy and always choose the plumpest ones.

Before soft-shells are eaten, they must be dressed (cleaned) - a simple process that can be done at home or you can have your fishmonger dress the crab.

Soft-shells can be kept in a paper bag in the refrigerator. Once the crab has been dressed (cleaned) the entire crab is edible. At this point, the soft-shells may also be frozen.

It is best to cook your soft-shells within 24 hours of purchasing; wait no longer than 48 hours. If your fishmonger cleaned the soft-shells, cook them within a few hours.

### Soft-shells Grading (Sizing)

| | |
|---|---|
| Whales | 5 ½ inches + |
| Jumbo | 5 - 5 ½ inches |
| Primes | 4 ½ - 5 inches |
| Hotels | 4 - 4 ½ inches |
| Mediums | 3 ½ - 4 inches. |

## Dressing (cleaning) Soft-shell Crab:

1. Using scissors, snip off the crabs' eyes and mouth; scoop out the soft material just behind this cut, and gently rinse the crab.

2. Lift the shell on each side of the body and, using your fingers or a small knife, remove the gray gills and discard them.

3. Lift up the "apron" (the flap of shell covering the belly of the crab) and twist or cut it off. The crab is now ready for cooking.

---

*When cooking (working) with crab, always be sure to thoroughly clean any area the crab has been; the resulting smell is not pleasant.*

## Fresh Crabmeat

Buying fresh crabmeat is a wonderfully convenient way to go, especially when you consider it would take about 20 blue crabs to get one pound of crabmeat. Dungeness crab fares better in that it would take 4 average sized crabs to obtain one pound of crabmeat (that's a lot of cleaning & picking!)

Dungeness crab is commonly packaged containing a combination of body, leg and claw meat. Blue crab is sold in grades (see chart) with wide price variations, lump being the most expensive and claw the least expensive. Although claw is the least expensive it is not inferior. Claw meat is very tasty and makes outstanding crab cakes and is a favorite for Gumbo. But, because of the darker coloration, its use is less desirable in dishes where appearance is essential.

Look for clear liquid in the packaging. Do not buy any seafood packed in murky or dark colored liquid. If possible, give it a good whiff.

> *If you ever find yourself short on crabmeat, shrimp is a great extender.*

### Blue crabmeat Grades

*Lump:* The largest pieces, solid morsels of white meat that come from the swimming or back legs. "Lump" is the most expensive. It is used in crab cocktails and salads. Use in recipes where appearance is important.

*Back Fin:* "Back fin" crabmeat comes from the body and legs of the crab. The pieces of meat are smaller than lump pieces. White body meat consists of lump and flakes. Pieces are smaller than lump, but can be substituted as lump meat

*Special:* "Special" crabmeat, is also known as regular, deluxe, flake, or white, and refers to smaller, white 'flake meat' from the entire body and center parts of the crab, as well as a minimum amount of back fin and jumbo lump. It always needs to be picked over carefully to remove any small pieces of shell.

*Claw:* Brownish tinged meat from the claws. It adds a rich flavor to gumbos and soups. Great in crab cake and dips. The least expensive type of crabmeat.

*Cocktail Claw:* This is the claw meat that has been left intact with part of claw pincer attached. Cocktail claws are great for cocktails or appetizers and make a dazzling presentation.

" There are two schools of thought about eating

cracked crab. There are those who eat the

crabmeat as fast as the shells are removed. Others

dig out all of the meat from their entire

portion, to eat at leisure when the work is done.

Adherents of the former procedure are invariably

scornful of those in the latter category, "

*-Helen Evens Brown*

# HOW TO HOST A CRAB FEAST

❧

There's just something about sitting around a table overflowing with crab that's just irresistible. It's sure to create a festive atmosphere for good friends and family I can't think of a more delightful way to spend an evening. It's just plain fun!

Your crab of choice would be either blue crab or Dungeness crab. If you will be serving blue crab plan on 6 per person with Dungeness 1 per person. No feast is complete without warm crusty sourdough bread. Other accompaniments you may want to include are serve red potatoes, corn on the cob, coleslaw and salad.

The Crab may be served hot or chilled, and if serving hot, melted butter for dipping is a necessity.

If chilled, cocktail and mayonnaise based sauces work well. Either way serve with lemons wedges. The crab can be served on a large platter or if serving Dungeness, you may want to place a crab on each guest's plate. If serving a Louisiana Crab Boil, its great fun just to dump it out in the middle of the table and let everyone dig in.

Cover the table with butcher paper or newspaper and set out plenty of napkins. You'll want to provide crab crackers or nutcrackers, crab forks or picks for extracting the meat, wooden mallets if you're serving blue crab for cracking the claws and containers to hold the discarded shells.

Always a lovely way to end the crab feast is to pass out warm hand-towels. You'll need one white wash cloth per person. To prepare the hand- towels ahead of time, dampen each one, roll it up and place on a tray or plate arranging them pyramid style. When everyone's finished; place the damp towels in the microwave for about 1 1/2 minutes or until very warm, then pass the plate or tray around the table allowing each person to take a hand-towel.

At the end of your crab feast, once all the silverware is accounted for simply roll up the newspaper and toss into the garbage. What could be easier?

## Frozen Crab

The main types of frozen crab you will encounter are king, snow and stone crab claws.

Avoid frozen crabmeat that appears freezer burned, dry, and yellowish tinged or discolored. However, don't be put off if the shells bear brownish or even black patches - these are simply signs of age and in no way influence the taste of the meat. The secret to retaining all the flavor and texture is a slow thaw (1 or 2 days) in the refrigerator. There are a variety of ways to reheat crab. Be careful not to overcook as it will toughen texture and diminish taste. To reheat stone crab simply steam 12 minutes. If serving the crab chilled, just thaw and serve. When serving crab in the shell that has already been cooked once, it is best not to re-heat in water. It is better to steam, roast, broil, grill or stir-fry.

## Pasteurized Crabmeat

Pasteurized crabmeat though not as good as fresh is a decent substitute. Pasteurized crabmeat is sold in hermetically sealed cans, usually with no preservatives or additives. The one exception is machine-picked claw meat, which uses a salt solution to separate the meat from the shell. Before using, always check for any stray pieces of cartilage or shell.

Pasteurized crabmeat will last up to six months when properly stored unopened in the coldest part of your refrigerator (usually the lowest shelf at the back or in the meat keeper). Once opened, use within three to four days.

## Canned Crabmeat

Canned crabmeat is available as claw meat, lump meat, or flaked meat. In terms of flavor and texture, canned crab is less desirable than pasteurized. Though this would typically be your last choice, there's a great convenience to always having crabmeat on hand. Most canned crabmeat is steamed and has been picked by machines rather than by hand. Crabmeat sold in stores must be labeled to indicate the origin of the crabmeat. It's better to purchase crab from the US. Canned crab is good for 6 months; once canned crab has been opened it should be treated as fresh and used within 3-4 days.

---

### Stone Crab Claw Sizes

**Medium claws:** good for appetizers (6 to 7 claws per pound).
For an appetizer, one pound per person should be considered.

**Large claws:** an excellent entrée (4 to 5 per pound).
For an appetizer, one pound should feed one person.
For an entrée, one and a half pounds per person.

**Jumbo claws:** an even better entrée (2 to 3 per pound).
Like the large claws, one and a half pounds should feed one person

**Colossal Claws:** now these are big!  7 ounces and over.

---

## FREEZING CRAB

You can freeze crabmeat in the shell or as crabmeat that was picked from its shell. Crabmeat must be cooked before freezing it, with soft-shell being the exception. Crab can be successfully frozen for several months, although I wouldn't recommend more than three.

I've had great success freezing Dungeness crab, both in the shell and the picked meat. When freezing crabmeat in solid portions, you may want to rinse any yellow "mustard" from the meat, as this may affect the flavor and the texture of the frozen meat. Blue crab is not recommended for freezing as the finely textured meat tends to toughen and dry out. Better results are obtained when frozen as part of a recipe. Stone crab should be frozen in the shell as the meat easily dries out. Soft-shell crab should always be cleaned before freezing and can be frozen alive. Freeze soft-shell crab individually. Frozen soft-shells are best served fried. I would not recommend sautéing or grilling soft-shells after freezing.

To freeze crabmeat, wrap it carefully in freezer paper or freezer plastic and over-wrap with a plastic freezer bag or if you have vacuum sealer all the better as that will aid in retaining moisture and freshness. Freeze for up to three months.

### Thawing Crab

A slow thaw in the refrigerator is always best. In a pinch, however, I've thawed crab in about 20 minutes in the sink with running cold water with good results. But a slow thaw is definitely the way to get the best flavor out of frozen crab. Here's how to do it:

1. Place the crab in your refrigerator on a baking pan with lots of newspaper under it, and let the crab drain as much liquid as possible as it thaws ( which may be as long as 2 days). You will find that the crab releases a lot of liquid during a thaw and you may need to change the newspaper several times. Uncleaned crab releases a great deal more liquid than cleaned. You can thaw crab in a plastic bag if you wish (less messy way).

2. When you're ready to use the crab, you can do one of two things, depending on your recipe.

*If your recipe calls for serving the crab in the shell,* go ahead and crack the crab and put it back in the refrigerator for another hour or two to further drain it before proceeding with your recipe.

*If you will be extracting the crabmeat from the shell for your recipe,* crack the crab, lay out fresh newspaper in the baking pan, and place the crabmeat on it to further thaw in the refrigerator (this is especially important if making crab cakes) to absorb the liquid. This may sound like a lot of work, but it is well worth the effort.

| Approximent crabmeat weight and measurement equivalents |
| --- |
| 4 ounces = about $^3/_4$ cup |
| 6 ounces = about 1 $^1/_8$ cups |
| 8 ounces = about 1 $^1/_2$ cups |
| 1 pound = about 3 cups |

**Reheating Crab**

There are a variety of ways to reheat crab. Be careful not to overcook as the texture will toughen and diminish taste. To reheat stone crab simply steam 12 minutes, if you will be serving the crab chilled, just thaw and serve. When serving crab in the shell that's already been cooked once, it's best not to re-heat in water. It's better to steam, roast, broil, grill or stir-fry.

*Fresh vs. Frozen*

Yes, there is no taste like crab that has been steamed or boiled fresh out of the pot. I had always read that fresh crab is far superior to frozen and I believed this for a long time. In fact, it was a frequent topic of debate between my husband (another one) and myself until one night we had guests coming for dinner, and not enough fresh crab so I had to pull some frozen out of the freezer. I was looking forward to proving once and for all that fresh is always better. I prepared Roasted Crab that night and kept the fresh separated from the frozen and guess what? Nobody including myself could taste the difference. But I have found there are steps you need to take in order to get the best flavor out of frozen crab. First, place crab in your refrigerator on a baking pan with lots of newspaper under it, you will find that the crab releases a lot of liquid and you may need to change the newspaper several times. (uncleaned crab releases a great deal more liquid than cleaned) You can thaw crab prior to this step in a plastic bag if you wish (less messy). When you're ready to use the crab go ahead and crack if your preparation is in the shell. Place back in refrigerator for an hour or two to further drain. If you will be extracting the crabmeat, you first crack the crab and place on newspaper and lay out fresh newspaper for the crabmeat I'll be extracting. Once you have all the crabmeat extracted leave it on the newspaper and place in the refrigerator to further drain (this is especially important if making crab cakes). This may sound like a lot of work but it is well worth the effort.

# HOW TO PICK A CRAB

*Carol Remsberg, who lives on the Eastern Shore of Maryland, has a web-site titled Tidewater Tales on which she posts her writings, most of which are personal essays. There are over a hundred and they're great fun to read. This essay was written in response to a reader's requesting information on how to 'shake' or 'shell a crab'. This covers seasoning, cooking, serving, and, in great detail, how to 'pick' (or separate the meat from the shell). With her permission, I am including the essay for your reference and enjoyment.*

Someone wrote me a little ways back about an article I'd written last summer. Oh, it was a nice "thank you" sort of thing, but it was also a plea for help. Her name is Kimberly. She was asking how to 'shake' or 'shell' a blue crab. Well, I'll admit I don't know how to 'shake or shell' but I do know how to 'pick' one. Her terms were more accurate although I've never called it anything else but "pickin'." At first I thought this would be an easy thing to explain. However without the visuals it can be difficult. My lack of artistic skills warrants some really in-depth explanations. So, Kimberly, if you will be patient I'll do my very best to be precise without the vocals and the mini-cam.

First of all there are a certain set of prerequisites that I will lay down before we even address the 'steamed' crab. Please note that I don't say 'boiled' or 'cooked' because those terms are for an even more southern way of cooking that will turn the delicate crabmeat of a Chesapeake Bay blue crab into mush or into something tough and inedible. Then there are the spices involved. So I must give you some guidelines or it isn't worth picking the crab to begin with. Of course you need a big pot to steam them, some water, not a huge amount—don't cover the crabs—an inch or two is plenty. You need some salt, some Old Bay seasoning or some Wye Mills Crab seasoning, a pint or two of vinegar, and a can or bottle of your favorite beer—you can pass on the beer if you like—it makes no real difference in the outcome, yet some folks swear by it.

This is for ½ to 1 bushel of lively crabs. Don't put a crab into the pot that doesn't try to pinch the hell out of you. A dead crab tastes nasty—no matter what you sprinkle on it or dip it into.

Put them in the pot, sprinkle liberally with seasoning—as they won't let you sprinkle much, smash the lid on and weight it down. Otherwise the feisty little buggers will scramble out of the pot. They aren't that stupid. Turn on the heat to full blast and steam for 15-20 minutes—not much more because if you do, they won't be worth eating.

Now dump them out upon a big back porch table covered heavily in old newspapers—it's cheaper that way. Go into the kitchen and melt some butter. Please notice that I didn't say margarine or oleo or any of that stupid fat-free stuff. I did say 'butter.' The salted kind is best. Put the melted butter into little bowls for dipping. You'll also need a second set of bowls for some cider vinegar. Yes, I did say 'cider vinegar.' This is also excellent for dipping your crabmeat into—yet most of us crack the claws and dump them in to soak up that vinegar for later consumption. It's awesome. My child cannot get enough.

Other accoutrements necessary for the table enabling easy consumption and full enjoyment are: several rolls of paper towels, one or two very large trash cans in close proximity—like standing next to said table, mallets or the reverse ends of heavy table knives to use as a hammer, and for each person a very good paring knife or something approximating that size. Oh, they have crab knives but you don't need them. A heavy-duty paring knife with a good edge is wonderful—just don't be clumsy or you'll end up slicing your tongue when you stick the meat in your mouth. You also need a firm hand and grip—nothing ventured, nothing gained. Picking crabs isn't for the frail or the timid.

Finally, do NOT forget your beverage of choice. Somehow iced tea doesn't do it. Even though I love iced tea, picking crabs is like playing in the mud. You have to get down and dirty—plenty of ice cold beer is a requirement. You will be at this table for a long time and it's not something that you sit and "go" from—at least not to anywhere else without a hot shower for the scent of crab lingers. Having good buddies and conversation will make this a memorable occasion. Remember this is an event—or should be if it's done properly.

**Now it's time to pick your crab. Sigh . . .!**

I've done everything I can do up to this point to avoid the actual dismemberment of a blue crab. Actually, it's very easy. However describing it is a challenge—even to a writer. I will take this step-by-step. Trust me, I'll bore you, but it will be very detailed.

First of all, please say you are right-handed because all of these instructions are for a 'righty' and not a 'lefty.' If you are a 'lefty' do the converse—or just bloody "go for it." Okay?

Lay that fat warm blue crab in your right hand. You put him in your right hand so that the thumb of your right hand rests upon the crab's left-end fin—the one that's rounded so the face of the crab faces you. (Are we being precise enough yet?)

Then, put your left hand across its body like an evangelist saying a prayer—you cover the whole crab with your hand. Your left thumb will instinctively loop around it's left point of the outer shell as if you want to rip it's top off. You are there! Press down with your right thumb and pull up with your left thumb. You will have parted that crab from his top shell. Now we are cookin' with gas.

Now what you will see is an ugly piece of business; the blue crab's innards. Don't worry, you don't have to play with that just yet. First, rip its legs off—all of them. During this procedure you will likely pull out a goodly chunk of meat—dip in either the butter or vinegar and plop it into your mouth. More work is ahead.

Once you've ripped his little legs off, then go for its face. Take that sharp knife and cut it away. No this isn't for the shy or the retiring—remember the little bugger is dead and won't feel a thing. Kids are great at this, most haven't learned any compassion yet. So think of someone you really hate and the rest will come easily.

Once you do this you are now staring at a smallish two-sided thingy with yucky stuff in the middle. Take that knife and scrape out all the loose stuff. Then you will notice the lungs or the "deadman's fingers" on the outer hull of those two sides. They lay on top of that inside of the shell—this is the only part really not recommended for consumption. Pull or scrape them off. Then, along the outer sides, cut away those knuckle joints with the knife. This is where most of your hand strength will come into play. Once this is done you will be really ready to get into the heart of the crab.

You have two sides. Go to the middle part that's empty of its innards and with your knife cut sideways to the outside. Do the same for the other side. You end up with three pieces. You'll have a bottom with two sides and two small tops. Then you take your sharp little knife and dig into the sides pulling out the delicate meat. With this meat upon your knife you can dip it in either the vinegar or the butter or simply into your mouth. The first few times you do this it will seem like a futile effort. Never fear, anyone can do this, it simply takes practice.

With time it can become second nature and loads of fun. With friends and family and a couple of beers you won't feel either inferior or inept. You'll simply relax and figure your own way to dig out the meat of the crab.

Please enjoy your crabs for they are special and close to my heart. The old days of plenty are gone. The Chesapeake Bay doesn't make what she used to and even when she does, those that devour them usually don't have to work for it any more. Wasting a crab is a crime—at least for me. Thank you Kimberly for reminding me.

# appetizers & starters

# APPETIZERS & STARTERS

baja crab & shrimp ceviche

crab & artichoke dip

crab & goat cheese empanadas

crab crostini

crab in endive spears

crab martini

crab rangoon

crab stuffed roasted poblanos with red bell pepper sauce

gruyere crab puffs

stone crab claws with mustard sauce

miniature crab cakes with roasted red pepper sauce

miniature crab spring rolls with dipping sauces

wild mushroom, crab and brie phyllo triangles

# baja crab & shrimp ceviche

*This is one of my all-time favorites—it's so refreshing. By definition, ceviche is an appetizer consisting of raw fish marinated in citrus juice. This, however, isn't ceviche in the truest sense of the word, because the seafood in this ceviche is cooked. I've found that serving this with warmed tortilla chips really enhances the flavors.*

2 tablespoons fresh-squeezed lemon juice
$^1/_2$ cup fresh-squeezed lime juice
4 scallions, finely chopped
$^1/_2$ red jalapeno pepper, stemmed, seeded and finely chopped
$^1/_2$ cup coarsely chopped cilantro leaves
1 teaspoon salt
$^1/_2$ teaspoon freshly ground black pepper
2 tablespoons olive oil
$^1/_2$ teaspoon garlic powder or $^1/_2$ teaspoon fresh minced garlic
$^1/_2$ teaspoon chili powder
$^1/_2$ teaspoon sugar
$^1/_2$ cup chopped cooked bay shrimp or other cooked shrimp
1 $^1/_2$ cups crabmeat
$^1/_2$ cup diced avocado
tortilla chips

**1.** Rinse the shrimp thoroughly with cold water.

**2.** Combine the lemon and lime juices, scallions, jalapeno pepper, cilantro leaves, salt, pepper, oil, garlic powder (or fresh garlic), chili powder and sugar in a medium bowl, and mix well. Add the shrimp, crabmeat and avocado, just enough to combine. Refrigerate the ceviche for 1 hour.

**3.** Preheat the oven to 225°. Arrange the tortilla chips on a cookie sheet, and warm them in the oven for 10 to 12 minutes before serving them with the ceviche.

*Note: **Sometimes you'll find that a large amount of liquid accumulates at the bottom of the ceviche while in the refrigerator. If this occurs, just drain some off before serving.***

# crab & artichoke dip

*Always a crowd pleaser. This dip is served in a hollowed-out bread bowl.*
*The dip can be prepared up to 2 days in advance and baked just before serving.*

2 cups crabmeat
8 ounces cream cheese, softened
2 cups mayonnaise
$^1/_3$ cup Dijon or wholegrain mustard
$^1/_4$ teaspoon ground cayenne pepper
$^1/_3$ cup white cheddar cheese (Pepper Jack also works well, if you like spicy)
$^1/_4$ cup grated Parmesan cheese
1 teaspoon garlic powder
dash Worcestershire sauce
1 (14-ounce) can artichoke hearts in water (not marinated), drained well and coarsely chopped
1 round loaf sourdough bread or Hawaiian bread, hollowed out, reserving bread cubes for serving

**1.** In a medium bowl, stir the cream cheese until smooth, and then beat in the mayonnaise until just blended. Fold in remaining ingredients until well mixed. If serving the dip at a later time, place in the refrigerator.

**2.** Heat the crab mixture in a medium saucepan, over low heat, until the cheese melts and the crab mixture is heated throughout.

**3.** Pour the crab dip into a hollowed out bread bowl and serve immediately, with bread cubes.

*Serves 6-8*

# crab & goat cheese empanadas

*Empanada is Spanish for "to bake in pastry." These freeze well as long as the crabmeat has not been previously frozen. You can also use frozen pie dough if you wish.*

**Pastry:**
2 ¹/₂ cups all-purpose flour
¹/₂ tablespoon salt
1 cup unsalted butter, chilled and cut into ¹/₂-inch cubes
1 egg, beaten
1 ¹/₂ tablespoons Champagne vinegar
¹/₃ cup ice water

**Filling:**
2 tablespoons butter
1 tablespoon oil
1 cup chopped scallions
¹/₄ cup finely chopped red pepper
1 clove garlic, minced
1 pound crabmeat
1 teaspoon salt
¹/₂ teaspoon freshly ground black pepper
2 tablespoons minced cilantro
1 cup soft goat cheese
1 egg white, beaten with 1 tablespoon water

***Prepare the Pastry:***
**1.** Combine the flour, salt and butter in a food processor. Run until it becomes a course meal. Add the egg and vinegar to the water, and then add this mixture to the processor. Process the mixture using the pulse function, until it forms a dough. Turn out the dough onto a lightly floured surface, and kneed gently, just enough to bring the dough together.

**2.** Roll out the dough into a rectangle, and then fold up the dough and wrap it in plastic wrap for at least 1 hour.

*Prepare the filling:*

**1.** In a medium saucepan, heat the butter and oil over medium-low heat. Add the scallions, red pepper and garlic, and sauté them until they are softened. Add the crabmeat, salt and pepper, and gently mix the filling until warmed.

**2.** In a large mixing bowl, fold the cilantro into the goat cheese, and then fold the crab mixture into it. Refrigerate until ready to use.

*Assembly:*

**1.** Preheat the oven to 325°.

**2.** Roll out the dough on a lightly floured surface, and make a rough circle about 1/8-inch thick.

**3.** With a 3-inch cookie cutter or glass, cut circles out of the dough. Place about 2 teaspoons of the crab mixture into the center of each circle. Wet your fingers in some water and moisten the exposed edges of the dough. Fold the empanadas in half, pressing the edges firmly together, and then crimp the edges together with the tines of a fork.

**4.** Brush the tops of the empanadas with the lightly beaten egg, and place on a lightly greased baking sheet. Bake for 15 to 20 minutes, until golden brown.

"Wine is sunlight, held together by water."
*-Galileo Galilei (1564-1642)*

# crab crostini

*This one is great when you're short on time; it's just so quick and easy.*
*You can make the crab mixture ahead of time and refrigerate until needed.*

8 ounces crabmeat
$^1/_2$ cup chopped roasted red bell pepper
3 tablespoons mayonnaise
2 teaspoons chopped fresh parsley
1 tablespoon fresh chives
1 tablespoon Dijon mustard
1 teaspoon parmesan cheese
1 tablespoon lime juice
3-5 drops hot pepper sauce

1 baguette cut into thin slices

**1.** Preheat the broiler. In a bowl, combine all ingredients except bread, and mix well. Spread 1 tablespoon of crab mixture on each slice of bread.

**2.** Place bread on baking sheet or broiler pan and broil 4 inches from heat 5 to 6 minutes or until lightly browned on top. Now wasn't that easy?

# crab in endive spears

*This dish tastes as delicious as it looks. When purchasing Belgian endive, look for large stalks that are creamy white, with pale yellow or green tips. The crab filling may be prepared up to 24 hours in advance. The endive should be prepared not long before serving, as the leaves tend to discolor.*

    4 heads Belgian endive*
    $1/4$ cup mayonnaise
    2 tablespoons minced chives
    1 tablespoon minced chives (garnish)
    1 tablespoon fresh lemon juice
    1 teaspoon lemon zest
    1 rib celery, finely chopped
    $1/2$ teaspoon salt
    $1/4$ teaspoon freshly ground black pepper
    1 cup crabmeat

Remove any damaged outer leaves from the endive and discard them. Cut about ¼ inch off the bottom (root) end, and carefully remove all the leaves. Separate and set aside 24 leaves.

### Prepare the Crab Filling:
In a medium bowl, combine the mayonnaise, chives, lemon juice, lemon zest, celery, salt, pepper and crabmeat. This can be prepared up 24 hours in advance.

### Assembly:
**1.** Place a tablespoon of the crab mixture on the wide end of each leaf.

**2.** Arrange spears on a serving plate in a starburst pattern, with tips pointing outward. Garnish the spears with minced chives, and serve.

**\* It is especially important for this recipe that the Belgian endive are fresh and firm.**

*Makes 24 Spears*

You can make this ahead and refrigerate it for 4 hours (cover with plastic wrap).

# crab martini

*The crab "martini" is an update on an old favorite, served in a martini glass and garnished with a crab claw clenching an olive. This is both elegant and fun.*

**Bloody Mary Cocktail Sauce**
$1/2$ cup tomato juice
1 teaspoon horseradish
$1/4$ cup chili sauce
$1/2$ teaspoon black pepper
dash of sugar
1 tablespoons fresh lemon juice
1 teaspoon Worcestershire sauce
1 tablespoon olive oil
2 teaspoons citron-flavored vodka or lemon-flavored vodka

1 cup chopped celery
1 pound crabmeat
2 scallions, mostly the green parts (garnish)
6 crab claws (garnish)
6 green olives
6 martini glasses

*Prepare the sauce:*
In a blender or food processor, puree the tomato juice, horseradish, chili sauce, pepper, sugar, lemon juice, Worcestershire sauce, olive oil and vodka. Refrigerate until ready to use.

*Assembly:*
Place some of the chopped celery in the bottom of each martini glass. Divide the crabmeat evenly among martini glasses, and then spoon the bloody Mary cocktail sauce over the crab. Garnish each serving with scallions and a crab claw clutching an olive.

*Note: The key to this recipe is for everything to be well chilled. I sometimes place the crab on ice for about 10 to 15 minutes prior to serving.*

*Serves 6*

# crab rangoon

*Although these seem to be a staple on the menu of many Chinese restaurants, crab Rangoon was actually the creation of a chef at Trader Vic's in the 1950's. This is the original Trader Vic's recipe. We can also thank Trader Vic's for the Mai Tai.*

$^1/_2$ pound crabmeat, well drained and chopped
$^1/_2$ pound cream cheese
$^1/_2$ teaspoon A1® Steak Sauce
$^1/_4$ teaspoon garlic powder
1 package wonton wrappers
1 egg yolk, well beaten
Chinese mustard

**1.** Combine the crabmeat with cream cheese, steak sauce and garlic powder in a medium bowl, and blend well.

**2.** Place 1 tablespoon of the crab mixture in the center of each wonton wrapper. For each wrapper, gather the edges together, moisten with egg yolk and pinch or twist to seal.

**3.** Heat the oil in an electric fry pan or skillet to 375°. Fry in bunches, until golden brown, about 3 minutes. Drain the wontons on paper towels. Serve hot with Chinese mustard.

*Makes 2$^1/_2$ to 3 dozen.*

# crab stuffed roasted poblanos with red bell pepper sauce

*Your guests will thank you. This dish makes a strikingly gorgeous display and the combination of flavors is superb. Have plenty of crusty bread on hand to soak up any red pepper sauce left. These can be assembled one day ahead and baked just prior to serving. These also make a great entrée, if serving as an entrée serve two per person.*

8 fresh poblano chilies *

**Filling:**
1 $^1/_2$ cups crabmeat or a combination of crabmeat
$^2/_3$ cup soft fresh goat cheese (about 4 ounces), room temperature
$^1/_2$ cup (packed) Pepper Jack cheese
$^1/_4$ cup chopped red bell pepper
2 tablespoons chopped shallot
2 $^1/_2$ tablespoons chopped fresh cilantro
2 $^1/_2$ tablespoons chopped fresh basil

**Red Bell Pepper Sauce:**
2-3 large red bell peppers*
1 tablespoon olive oil
$^1/_4$ cup chopped shallots
2 garlic cloves, minced
1 jalapeno pepper, seeded, minced
$^1/_2$ teaspoon cayenne
$^1/_8$ teaspoon sugar
1 cup low-salt chicken broth

*Make Sauce:*
**1.** Char bell peppers over gas flame or in broiler until blackened on all sides. Enclose in plastic bag 10 minutes. Peel, seed, and coarsely chop bell peppers.

**2.** Heat oil in medium skillet over medium heat. Add shallots, garlic, and chili; sauté until shallots are soft, about 5 minutes.

**3.** Transfer mixture to blender; add bell peppers and chicken broth, cayenne and sugar. Puree until smooth. Season to taste with salt and pepper. (Can be made 1 day ahead, refrigerate and re-heat before serving.)

Char poblano chilies over gas flame or in broiler until blackened on all sides. Enclose in paper bag 10 minutes. Peel chilies. Using small sharp knife, carefully slit chilies open along 1 side. Remove seeds, leaving stems attached. Set aside

*Assembly:*
**1.** Mix cheeses, red pepper, shallot, cilantro and basil in medium bowl. Season to taste with salt and pepper. Fold in crab and mix gently.

**2.** Fill chilies with crab mixture, dividing equally. Pull up sides of chilies to enclose filling. Place stuffed chilies on baking sheet, cover and refrigerate if not serving immediately.

**3.** Bake at 350 for 15 minutes.(if the stuffed chilies have been previously refrigerated add 3-4 minutes)

*To Serve:*
Spoon about $^1/_4$ to $^1/_3$ cup red bell pepper sauce onto 8 plates. Place one stuffed chili atop sauce on each plate and serve.

*Makes 8 Servings appetizer servings or 4 entrée servings.*

**\* Poblanos are sometimes called pasillas.**
**\* You may also use roasted red bell peppers from a jar.**

# gruyere crab puffs

*These are melt-in-your-mouth delicious.*
*These can be made ahead of time and popped in the oven just before serving.*

**Filling:**
$1/2$ cup crabmeat
$1/2$ cup grated Gruyere cheese
$1/4$ cup minced scallions

**Puffs:**
$1/2$ cup beer (preferably lager) or water
4 tablespoons butter
$1/2$ teaspoon salt
$1/2$ cup flour
2 eggs, at room temperature

*Note: **You can make the puffs (unfilled) a day ahead; keep them at room temperature in an airtight container. Once filled they can sit in the refrigerator a few hours before baking**.*

Preheat the oven to 375°.

*Prepare the puffs:*
**1.** Heat the beer (or water), butter and salt in a medium saucepan over medium heat. As soon as the mixture comes to a boil, remove from heat, and quickly **add the flour, all at once.** Vigorously stir the mixture with a wooden spoon, until it leaves the sides of the pan and forms a smooth ball. Remove the dough from the heat and let it cool for about 5 minutes.

**2.** Add eggs, 1 at a time, beating hard until the mixture is smooth and glossy after each addition (about 1 minute). Drop the mixture by rounded tablespoons onto a greased baking sheet, leaving 2 inches between the puffs to permit spreading.

**3.** Bake the puffs for about 30 minutes, or until they are golden brown. (leave the oven on)

**4.** Prepare the filling: Toss together the crabmeat, gruyere cheese and scallions in a medium bowl.

*Assembly:*
Slice the top off each puff. Gently pull out the moist dough out of the center and discard. Fill each puff with crab mixture. Bake until the cheese has melted about 5-10 minutes.
Serve immediately.

*Makes 3 to 4 dozen*

# stone crab claws with mustard sauce

*The Stone crab claws are purchased fully cooked and may be frozen or thawed,*
*if given a choice always choose the frozen claws, as you don't know when they were thawed,*
*always better to do it yourself. Plan on serving 3 claws per person.*

12- 15 stone crab claws
2 lemons cut into wedges

**Mustard Sauce:**
$1/2$ cup sour cream
$1/2$ cup mayonnaise
$1/2$ cup spicy brown mustard
1 tablespoon honey
$3/4$ tablespoon Worcestershire sauce
1 teaspoon dry mustard

*Prepare mustard sauce:*
Combine all ingredients in a small bowl and stir until well-blended. Refrigerate until ready to use.

Crack crab claws using a mallet, strike the shell at the main section then turn the claw and crack each knuckle at the side.

*To Serve:*
Cover large platter with crushed ice. Place mustard sauce in the middle. Arrange crab claws and lemon wedges on crushed ice.

# miniature crab cakes with roasted red pepper sauce

*Panko bread crumbs give these crab cakes a deliciously crispy crust. You'll find panko bread crumbs in the Asian section of your market. The crab cake mixture can be prepared a day ahead and cooked just before you are ready to serve them. The sauce may also be prepared a day ahead. The crab cakes may be served warm or at room temperature.*

**Roasted Red Pepper Sauce:**
1 cup mayonnaise
1 (8-ounce) jar fire-roasted red peppers
1 tablespoon fresh lemon juice
$1/4$ teaspoon ground cayenne pepper
$1/4$ cup sliced almonds
1 teaspoon garlic powder

**Crab Cakes:**
$1/3$ cup mayonnaise
1 egg, beaten
2 teaspoons Dijon mustard
$1/4$ cup finely minced red pepper
2 tablespoons finely minced chives
$1/2$ teaspoon salt
$1/4$ teaspoon freshly ground black pepper
$1/4$ teaspoon ground cayenne pepper
1 pound crabmeat, excess moisture squeezed out
$1/4$ cup panko bread crumbs
1 cup panko bread crumbs on a medium plate or pie tin
3 tablespoons oil
3 tablespoons butter
lemon wedges (garnish)

*Prepare Roasted Red Pepper Sauce:*
Combine the mayonnaise, red peppers, lemon juice, cayenne pepper, almonds and garlic powder in a blender or food processor, and blend (or process) the ingredients until smooth.

Refrigerate the sauce until you are ready to serve.

***Prepare Crab Cakes:***

**1.** Whisk the mayonnaise, egg, mustard, red pepper, chives, salt, pepper and cayenne pepper in a large bowl. Gently fold in the crabmeat and panko bread crumbs with a spatula (you may also use your hands). Refrigerate the crab mixture for at least 1 hour, up to 1 day (refrigerating the crab mixture helps to keep their shape and prevents them from falling apart when cooking).

**2.** Shape the crab mixture into about 24 cakes, each about 2 inches wide and a 1/2 inch thick. Gently turn each cake into the panko bread crumbs, coating the cakes evenly.

**3.** Heat the oil and butter in a large skillet over medium-low heat. Add the crab cakes, cooking them for 2 minutes on each side, until they are lightly browned. Serve the crab cakes on a platter with the lemon wedges, and roasted red pepper sauce.

*Makes 24 crab cakes*

# miniature crab spring rolls
## with dipping sauces

*These crispy little spring rolls are just delectable. One bit of advice:*
*make more than you think you will need, because these go fast.*

**Spring Rolls:**
1 tablespoon sesame seeds
salt to taste
3 tablespoons chopped scallion
1 tablespoon finely chopped red pepper
2 egg whites, lightly beaten, divided
$1/2$ teaspoon ginger
1 pound crabmeat
salt to taste
freshly ground black pepper to taste
1 package mini spring roll wrappers (or regular size, cut in half diagonally)
peanut oil or vegetable oil (1 tablespoon plus enough for frying)
15 butter lettuce leaves to line platter (rolls can also be served wrapped in leaves)

Sweet chili sauce*

**Sesame-Ginger Sauce:**
$1/3$  cup soy sauce
1 teaspoon Chinese hot mustard (or more if you like it hotter)
1 tablespoon sugar
1 teaspoon Asian sesame oil
1 teaspoon ginger powder
2 tablespoons lemon juice (optional)
2 tablespoons lime juice (optional)

*Prepare the Sesame-Ginger Dipping sauce:*
Pour the soy sauce into a small bowl, and whisk in the mustard, sugar, oil, ginger, lemon juice
and lime juice.

*Prepare the Spring Rolls:*

**1.** Toast the sesame seeds with the salt, in a small dry skillet over moderate heat, for about 2 minutes, until the seeds are golden. Transfer them to a medium bowl.

**2.** Heat 1 tablespoon of oil in the same pan over medium heat, and then add the scallions and red pepper, cooking them until softened. Add the cooked vegetables, egg white and ginger powder to the bowl with the sesame seeds. Gently fold in the crabmeat. Season to taste with salt and pepper.

*Assembly:*

**1.** Spread 1 tablespoon of crab mixture uniformly along one edge of the wrapper, allowing space at each end for folding in.

**2.** Roll the wrapper as tightly as possible, and at the halfway point, tuck the sides in. Seal the seam by brushing it with the egg white. Keep the remaining wrappers covered to prevent them from drying. Repeat this process until all the filling has been used.

*Cooking:*

Add enough oil to a large skillet to cover the rolls about halfway. Heat to medium-high, until oil is sizzling hot but not smoking, about 360°. Slowly place the rolls in the oil, seam-side down, careful not to crowd. Cook them until they become golden brown on each side.

*To serve:*

Line a serving platter with lettuce leaves and place the dipping sauces in the center. Arrange the spring rolls on top of the lettuce leaves.

***This type of sauce is available in the Asian section at your market (I use the Maggi® brand).***

*Serves 6-8*

# wild mushroom, crab and brie phyllo triangles

*A great make-ahead appetizer, this sublime appetizer is just oozing with taste. They also freeze well. Instead of making small triangles, you can also make large ones for individual appetizer servings.*

$3/4$ cup crabmeat, well-drained
2 tablespoons butter
2 cups diced porcini and crimini mushrooms*
$1/4$ cup chopped shallots
$1/2$ teaspoon salt
$1/4$ teaspoon freshly ground black pepper
4 cloves garlic, minced
1 roll phyllo pastry sheets**
$1/2$ cup melted butter
8 ounces brie cheese

### Prepare the filling:

**1.** Melt the butter in a medium skillet over low heat. Add the mushrooms, shallots, salt, pepper and garlic, sautéing them until they are softened and all the liquid is evaporated.

**2.** Remove the mushroom mixture from the heat and place them in the refrigerator to cool.

### Assembly:

**1.** Preheat the oven to 350°.

**2.** Unroll the phyllo sheets and cover them with plastic wrap and a damp towel. Place 1 phyllo sheet on your work surface, brush it lightly with melted butter, and cut it into 3-inch strips, lengthwise.

**3.** At the bottom end of one strip, place about a $1/2$ teaspoon of brie cheese. Place about 1 teaspoon of crab on top of the brie, and top the crab with about 1 teaspoon of the mushroom mixture.

**4.** Fold one corner of phyllo diagonally across to the opposite edge, to form a triangle, pressing mixture with your finger to evenly spread. Continue to fold triangle unto itself, (like folding a flag). Brush lightly with melted butter. Repeat with remaining phyllo sheets. If you are making these ahead of time, cover the triangles tightly with plastic, and refrigerate them until you are ready to bake.

**5.** Place each triangle, seam-side down, at least 1 inch apart, on an ungreased cookie sheet. Bake for about 15 to 20 minutes, until golden brown.

*Makes 10 to 12 small triangles or 4 large triangles*

***Mushrooms - Any variety may be used, including white button mushrooms.***

****You won't need the whole phyllo dough roll for this recipe; however, I find it easier to work with a roll, than trying to separate several sheets from a folded stack. Also, it's good to have extra. Phyllo dough can be re-frozen.***

### Tips on working with Phyllo:

Phyllo dough dries out quickly once it is exposed to air. Do not remove it from the package until you are ready to use the dough. Once it is removed from the package, cover it with plastic wrap and a damp towel. To prevent the edges from cracking, brush them with butter first then work into center. Fillings for phyllo dough should be chilled and not excessively moist.

# lunch, brunch & salads

# LUNCH, BRUNCH & SALADS

artichoke, potato and crab frittata

bayou soft- shell po' boy

california roll salad

cilantro lime crab stuffed avacado

classic crab louis

crab confetti salad

crab melt

crab benedict with key lime hollandaise sauce

green chile & crab quiche

mrs. ritchie's prize winning souffle

savory crab & red potato hash

spicy lemon crab cakes on mixed greens

# artichoke, potato and crab frittata

*A frittata is an Italian omelet. In Italy, frittatas are generally served as an appetizer,*
*light lunch or supper. Serve with fruit and some good bread, and you've got a wonderful meal!*
*This is my daughter's all-time favorite.*

3 medium red potatoes or 1 small russet, cut into $\frac{1}{2}$-inch dice

$\frac{1}{4}$ cup chopped shallots

1 teaspoon minced fresh rosemary or $\frac{1}{2}$ teaspoon dried rosemary

2 tablespoons olive oil

$\frac{3}{4}$ cup chopped artichoke hearts

8 ounces crabmeat

8 large eggs

$\frac{1}{2}$ teaspoon salt

$\frac{1}{4}$ teaspoon freshly ground black pepper

3 or 4 drops hot sauce

$\frac{1}{2}$ cup finely grated Parmesan cheese, reserving 3 tablespoons

2 tablespoons butter

**1.** Adjust oven rack to the upper-middle position and preheat the broiler.

**2.** Sauté the potato, shallots and rosemary in oil, over medium-low heat for about 5 minutes, until softened. Add the artichoke hearts and cook for another minute. Remove the mixture from the heat and gently fold in the crabmeat.

**3.** In a large bowl, whisk together the eggs, salt, pepper and hot sauce. Add the cheese (reserving 3 tablespoons), and combine the egg mixture with the crab mixture.

**4.** Heat the butter in a 10-inch non-stick skillet over medium heat. When it begins to foam, add the egg-and-crab mixture. Turn heat to low. Swirl the skillet to evenly distribute the ingredients. When the bottom has set and is golden, and when only the surface is runny, remove the frittata from the heat. Sprinkle the reserved cheese over the top.

**5.** Place the frittata under the broiler until it becomes puffed and golden in color, about 2 to 4 minutes. Loosen the frittata gently with a spatula until it moves freely in the pan, and then slide it out onto a platter. Cut the frittata into wedges and serve.

*Serves 4-6*

# bayou soft-shell po' boy

*It just doesn't get better than this—crunchy, juicy soft-shell crab served on a French roll, slathered with tartar sauce, with crisp lettuce and juicy tomato.*

**Tartar sauce:**

1 cup mayonnaise

1 teaspoon Worcestershire sauce

1 teaspoon Dijon mustard

2 tablespoons tiny capers

2 tablespoons lemon juice

3 tablespoons sweet pickle relish

2 tablespoons minced shallots or onions

$1/4$ teaspoon hot sauce

**Crab:**

$3/4$ cup flour

1 teaspoon salt

$1/2$ teaspoon freshly ground black pepper

3 tablespoons butter

3 tablespoons oil

$3/4$ cup milk

4 soft-shell crabs, cleaned

**Sandwich fixings:**

4 French rolls, toasted

lettuce leaves

tomato slices

***Prepare the Tartar sauce:***

Blend the mayonnaise, Worcestershire sauce, mustard, capers, lemon juice, relish, shallots (or onions) and hot sauce. Refrigerate the sauce for at least 1 hour. This will keep in the refrigerator for up to 1 week.

***Prepare the crab:***

Mix the flour, salt and pepper in a shallow bowl or plate. Heat the butter and oil in a large skillet over medium-high heat. Dip the crab in milk and then dredge it in flour. Sauté the crab, top-side down, for about 2 minutes. Then sauté the other side for another minute. Drain on a plate lined with paper towels or newspaper.

***To Serve:***

Place each soft-shell crab on a French roll. Top with tartar sauce, lettuce and tomato.

*Serves 4*

*The po' boy has a mixed history, with several theories regarding its origins. The most accepted is that in the 1920s, the po' boy sandwich was created by two brothers, Clovis and Benjamin Martin, at their New Orleans restaurant in the French Market. During a local transit worker's strike, the two brothers took pity on those "poor boys". Some say they were free for the "Poor boys".*

# *california roll salad*

*Light, refreshing and slightly spicy, this salad tastes just like a California roll,
but without all the work. It's especially great on a summer day.*

1 $\frac{1}{2}$ cups short grain sushi rice (you can also use long grain rice)
$\frac{1}{4}$ cup rice vinegar (unseasoned)
3 tablespoons canola or other mild oil
$\frac{1}{4}$ cup of sugar
1 teaspoon salt
$\frac{2}{3}$ cup peeled and grated carrot
2 tablespoons coarsely chopped Japanese sliced pickled ginger
$\frac{1}{4}$ cup minced scallions
1 large seedless cucumber, quartered and chopped
1 tablespoon and 2 teaspoons black sesame seeds (reserved)
1 $\frac{1}{2}$ sheets toasted nori sheets (dried laver) cut into thin strips with scissors*
1 avocado, cut crosswise into $\frac{1}{4}$ inch slices
1 pound of crabmeat
2 tablespoons Masago** (optional)

**Wasabi Dressing:**
3 teaspoons wasabi powder
4 tablespoons warm water
2 $\frac{1}{2}$ tablespoons soy sauce
2 teaspoons ginger juice (from pickled ginger jar)

**1.** Rinse the rice well in cold water, until the water is almost clear (this prevents the rice from tasting starchy). Cook the rice and set aside to cool.

**2.** Whisk the rice vinegar, oil, sugar and salt in a small bowl, until the sugar dissolves. Transfer the rice to a large bowl and stir in the vinegar mixture. Add the carrot, ginger, scallions, cucumber, sesame seeds (reserving the 2 teaspoons), ¾ of the nori, and the avocado, and combine. Add the crabmeat.

*Make Dressing:*
Mix the wasabi powder, water, soy sauce and ginger juice
together in a small bowl, until smooth.

*To Serve:*
 Give the salad another toss if it has been refrigerated and add remaining ingredients: nori, avocado, crab, and dressing. Garnish the salad with remaining nori, sesame seeds and Masago. If you would like to serve this on plates, rather than in bowls, line plates with mixed salad greens (spinach also works well).

*\* If you're short on time, the nori can also be crumbled.*

*\*\*Masago is Icelandic caviar. It's a brilliant orange, with a delicate mild flavor. It's slightly crunchy and almost seems to pop in your mouth.*

*Serves 4-6*

*Note:* **Part of the salad may be prepared—without the dressing, nori, avocado and crabmeat—up to 24 hours in advance**.

# cilantro lime crab stuffed avocado

*This simple, summery dish of avocado halves filled with
crabmeat makes a delightful lunch or first course.*

$^1/_4$ cup mayonnaise
3 tablespoons fresh lime juice, reserving 1 tablespoon for brushing
2 tablespoons minced red bell pepper
$^1/_4$ teaspoon ground cayenne pepper
$^1/_4$ cup chopped scallions (mostly the white part)
salt
freshly ground black pepper
1 pound crabmeat
2-3 large ripe avocados
2 tablespoons minced cilantro
lime wedges

### Crab Mixture:

In a medium bowl, whisk together the mayonnaise, lime juice, bell pepper, cayenne pepper
and scallions. Season to taste with salt and pepper. Gently fold in the crab with a spatula.
Refrigerate the crab mixture for at least 1 hour prior to serving.

### To Serve:

**1.** Halve the avocados, carefully removing the pits using a large spoon. Brush the cut surface
with the lime juice, to prevent discoloration.

**2.** Fill the avocado halves with the crab mixture. Garnish each serving with cilantro and a
lime wedge.

*Serves 4-6*

# classic crab louis

*Pronounced LOO-ey. The origin of the classic crab Louis is claimed by both the Olympic Club in Seattle and the St. Francis Hotel in San Francisco. There are many versions of this salad. The original simply called for lettuce, crabmeat, hard-boiled egg, and a simple mayonnaise dressing. This is my version.*

**Louis Dressing:**
1 cup mayonnaise (homemade or store bought)
1/4 cup chili sauce
3 tablespoons minced scallions
1 tablespoon lemon juice
1 teaspoon Worcestershire sauce
pinch ground cayenne pepper
1/4 teaspoon salt
1/2 teaspoon freshly ground black pepper

1 head iceberg lettuce, shredded
2 cups crabmeat
3 hard-boiled eggs, cut into wedges
2 tomatoes, cut into wedges
1 avocado, cut into wedges
2 lemons, cut into wedges

*Note: The dressing on the side is a personal preference. The crab itself can be mixed with a small amount of dressing. Also, the lettuce can be mixed with the dressing prior to putting it on the plates.*

*Make Dressing:*
Whisk together the mayonnaise, chili sauce, scallions, lemon juice, Worcestershire sauce, cayenne pepper, salt and pepper in a large bowl. Refrigerate the dressing for at least 1 hour.

*Assembly:*
**1.** Place the shredded iceberg on plates. Mound the crab on top of the lettuce. Garnish with egg, tomatoes, avocado and lemon wedges, around the sides of each plate, alternating as you go.

**2.** Serve the dressing on the side.

*Serves 4*

# crab benedict with
# key lime hollandaise sauce

*Delightfully decadent, eggs Benedict dates back to the 1920's. The hollandaise sauce in this recipe is made in a blender and is absolutely fool-proof. The key lime flavor adds a delicious new twist to this classic breakfast dish. Fresh minced chives add the perfect finishing touch.*

**Key Lime Hollandaise Sauce:**
1 cup butter
3 egg yolks
$1/2$ teaspoon salt
dash of cayenne pepper
2 tablespoons key lime juice (regular limes may be used, or lemons, if you prefer)

4 eggs
1 tablespoon vinegar (for poaching)
2 English muffins, split and toasted
8 ounces crabmeat, warmed
minced chives

*Prepare Hollandaise sauce:*
Melt the butter over medium heat until bubbling, being careful not to brown. Place egg yolks, salt and pepper in a blender or food processor. Blend at high speed for a few seconds, until you have a smooth frothy mixture. Still at a high speed, start adding the hot butter in a thin steady stream. The sauce will start thickening as you add the butter. When half the butter has been added, add the lime juice (or lemon juice). Continue until all the butter has been used.

*Poach eggs:*
**1.** In a large non-stick skillet, add the water within 1 inch from the top. Bring the water to a slow boil.

**2.** Add the vinegar. Break each egg into a small custard cup or small bowl. Swirl the water and quickly release the egg. Spoon cooking water over the top as they cook, for just 3 to 5 minutes, and they're done!

**3.** Toast the English muffins while the eggs poach. When the eggs are done, remove them with a spatula (I know it's generally done with a slotted spoon, but I've found that a spatula works better at keeping the egg whole). Sprinkle with salt and pepper.

*Assembly:*
Place 1 toasted English muffin on a plate, place some crabmeat on it, and then place a poached egg on top. Spoon the hollandaise over the top and sprinkle minced chives for the garnish. Voila!

*Serves 4*

"A good cook is like a
sorceress who dispenses happiness."
*-Elsa Schiaparelli*

# crab confetti salad

*This salad is also wonderful as a sandwich filling on sourdough bread,*
*or stuffed in avocado or tomato halves.*

$^1/_3$ cup of homemade mayonnaise, or Best Foods® or Hellmann's® mayonnaise
$^1/_4$ cup sour cream
1 teaspoon of concentrated tomato paste*
1 teaspoon Old Bay® Seasoning
$^1/_4$ teaspoon of freshly ground black pepper
1 pound of crabmeat
$^1/_3$ cup minced red and yellow bell pepper
$^1/_4$ cup of minced shallots (red onion may be substituted)

In a medium bowl, mix the mayonnaise, sour cream, tomato paste, Old Bay® Seasoning and pepper until well blended. Add the crab, red and yellow pepper and shallots. Gently mix. This is best refrigerated at least 1 hour before serving.

***The tomato paste I use comes in a tube and can be refrigerated. I find the flavor to be far superior to the canned variety. Two brands I've used and recommend are Amore® and Parma® Panocchia. I've found it also adds a wonderful richness and flavor to sauces and soup**s.

*Serves 4-6*

# crab melt

*I can't think of a more satisfying lunch. This is also good as an appetizer on baguettes.*

$1/2$ cup mayonnaise
1 tablespoons lemon juice
1 teaspoon Old Bay® Seasoning
$1/2$ teaspoon hot sauce
$1/4$ teaspoon freshly ground black pepper
3 scallions chopped (all of white and most of green)
1 pound crabmeat
salt
freshly ground pepper
4 thick slices sourdough or Italian bread
4 thin slices white cheddar cheese

**1.** Position a rack in the upper third of the oven. Preheat the oven to 425° .

**2.** Whisk together the mayonnaise, lemon juice, Old Bay® Seasoning, hot sauce, and  black pepper in a small bowl. Add the scallions. Pour the mixture over the crab and toss to coat. Season to taste with salt and pepper. Refrigerate for at least 30 minutes.

***Assembly:***
**1.** Lightly toast the bread.

**2.** Spread the crab mixture evenly over the bread slices. Top each bread slice with cheese, and place them on a baking sheet. Bake for about 5 to 8 minutes, until the cheese is bubbly. Turn the oven to broil, and cook them until the cheese begins to brown (watch closely so that the cheese does not burn).

*Serves 4*

# green chile & crab quiche

*Crab and green chiles complement each other wonderfully in this tasty quiche.*
*The green chiles arranged in a sunburst pattern on top of the quiche makes for a beautiful presentation.*

1 tablespoon oil
$^1/_2$ cup chopped scallions (all of white and most of green)
3 eggs, beaten
5 ounces light cream
3 to 5 drops hot sauce
$^1/_2$ teaspoon salt
$^1/_4$ teaspoon freshly ground black pepper
1 cup crabmeat (well-drained)
1 frozen (9-inch) pie shell, or your own homemade pie shell
$^1/_2$ cup green chilies, fresh or canned, chopped
$^3/_4$ cup Pepper Jack cheese, grated
2 whole green chiles (fresh or canned), cut into strips

**1.** Preheat the oven to 375°.

**2.** Sauté the scallions in 1 tablespoon of oil, until it is softened.

**3.** Whisk together the eggs, light cream, hot sauce, salt and pepper. Set the mixture aside.

**4.** Spread the crab evenly over the bottom of pie shell. Use half of the chopped chiles to make a layer over the crab, and then add a layer of cheese, another layer of chiles, another layer of cheese, and then the scallions. Pour the egg mixture over the scallions. Arrange the green chile strips in a sunburst pattern on the top.

**5.** Bake for about 35 minutes, until the center is set.

*Serves 6*

# mrs. ritchie's prize winning soufflé

*In 1954, Mrs. O.T. Ritchie won a $500 grand prize with this recipe in
The Seattle Times Annual Recipe Contest. This recipe continues to be requested today.
In 2003, the Soufflé was chosen as one of the 10 best recipes of the year.*

1 onion, peeled and finely chopped
1 green bell pepper, stemmed, seeded and chopped
1 cup chopped celery
1 tablespoon butter
8 slices white bread
2 cups cooked crab or shrimp meat
$^1/_2$ cup mayonnaise
3 cups milk
4 eggs
1 can (10¾ ounces) mushroom soup
About 1½ cups grated cheddar
Paprika

**1.** Cook onion, bell pepper and celery in the butter for a few minutes to soften. Set aside to cool.

**2.** Dice half of the bread into a 2½-quart baking dish. Mix crab or shrimp with mayonnaise and vegetables and spread over diced bread. Trim crusts from remaining bread slices and place over seafood mixture. Mix milk and eggs and pour over mixture. Cover and place in refrigerator overnight.

**3.** Remove cover and place baking dish in a preheated 325-degree oven for 15 minutes. Take from oven and spoon soup over top. Sprinkle cheese and paprika on top. Continue baking 1 hour. Remove from oven and cool 10 minutes before serving.

***\* If you prefer not to use canned soup, white sauce (see sauces and salsas) may be substituted, or this can be skipped altogether.***

*Serves 8-12*

# savory crab & red potato hash

*This recipe comes from Melissa Coray and Nicole Wergeland, chefs and owners of the Oval Door Bed & Breakfast Inn in Eugene, Oregon. The cream cheese sauce in this hash adds a wonderful creaminess to the dish. I've made the addition of the peppers, for added color and flavor.*

2 pounds red or boiling potatoes, peeled and cut into $^3/_4$-inch pieces
6 slices bacon
1 onion, chopped
1 small red pepper, cut into $^1/_2$-inch dice (about $^1/_2$ cup)
1 small green pepper, cut into $^1/_2$-inch dice (about $^1/_2$ cup)

$^1/_2$ teaspoon salt, divided
3 ounces cream cheese
$^1/_4$ cup milk
1 $^1/_2$ teaspoons Worcestershire sauce
pinch ground cayenne pepper

$^3/_4$ pound Dungeness crabmeat
$^1/_4$ teaspoon freshly ground black pepper
3 tablespoons chopped scallion tops
$^1/_4$ cup grated Parmesan cheese

4 poached or fried eggs (optional)

**1.** Place potatoes into a large pot of water, and bring it to a boil. Reduce the heat and simmer, until almost tender (about 5 minutes). Drain the potatoes.

**2.** Cook the bacon until crisp in a large skillet. Remove the bacon and crumble it. Pour off and reserve all but about 1 tablespoon the fat from the pan. Add the onion and peppers, and sauté them over medium heat until browned, stirring frequently. Remove the onion and peppers, and wipe the pan.

**3**. In the same pan, heat the reserved bacon fat over medium heat. Add the potatoes, and let them cook without stirring for 6 minutes. Add 1/4 teaspoon of salt, and stir and cook the potatoes until they are well browned, about 6 minutes longer. Add the onion and bacon, and continue cooking until they are warmed through, about 1 minute longer.

**4.** In a medium saucepan, heat the cream cheese, milk, Worcestershire sauce, cayenne pepper, and remaining $1/4$ teaspoon of salt, stirring over low heat, until hot. Add the crabmeat and black pepper, and continue stirring until heated through, about 2 more minutes.

**5.** Stir the crab mixture into the potatoes, along with the chopped scallions and Parmesan cheese, until just combined. Serve hot. If desired, top with eggs.

*Serves 4*

# spicy lemon crab cakes on mixed greens

*These sensational crab cakes are served on mixed greens with a creamy lemon vinaigrette that's drizzled over the top of the crab cakes and greens. These crab cakes are also marvelous served on their own, with any of the sauces or salsas listed in Chapter 6.*

**Creamy Lemon Vinaigrette:**

1 shallot, minced
$^1/_2$ cup fresh lemon juice
1 tablespoon grated lemon peel
1 tablespoon champagne vinegar
$^1/_2$ teaspoon Dijon mustard
$^1/_2$ teaspoon sugar
$^3/_4$ teaspoon salt
$^1/_4$ teaspoon freshly ground black pepper
$^1/_4$ cup canola oil
$^1/_4$ cup extra virgin olive oil

**Crab Cakes:**

$^1/_3$ cup mayonnaise
1 egg, beaten
2 teaspoons prepared horseradish
1 teaspoon dry mustard
1 teaspoon Old Bay® Seasoning
1 teaspoon grated lemon peel
1 tablespoon lemon juice
$^1/_4$ teaspoon ground cayenne pepper
1 pound crabmeat
$^1/_2$ cup finely crushed saltine crackers
3 tablespoons oil
3 tablespoons butter

**Salad:**

$^1/_4$ cup mixture of fresh basil
4 cups mixed baby greens

*Creamy Lemon Vinaigrette:*
Combine the shallots, lemon juice, lemon peel, vinegar, mustard, sugar, salt and pepper in a blender on low speed, and then slowly add the oil in a slow stream, blending until an emulsion forms. Stop blending once all the oil has been added. Taste and adjust the seasoning if needed.

*Crab Cakes:*
**1**. Whisk together the mayonnaise, egg, horseradish, mustard, Old Bay® Seasoning, lemon peel, lemon juice and cayenne pepper in a large bowl. Gently fold in the crabmeat and saltine crackers. Using a spatula, mix gently just to combine. Refrigerate the mixture for at least 2 hours, up to 1 day.

**2.** Shape the crab mixture into 8 small or 4 large crab cakes (I like to serve 2 per salad). Heat the oil and butter in a large skillet over medium-low heat. Add the crab cakes, cooking them until they turn a light golden brown.

*Assembly:*
Divide greens and basil among 4 plates, top with crab cakes. Drizzle lemon dressing over greens and crab cakes.

*Serves 4*

# soups, chowders & bisque

# SOUPS, CHOWDERS & BISQUE

*charleston she-crab soup*

*cajun crab & shrimp gumbo*

*cognac- laced crab bisque*

*dungeness crab, red potato and corn chowder*

*santa fe gazpacho*

*brazilian crab soup*

*thai coconut crab soup*

"Do you have a kinder, more adaptable friend in the food world than soup? Who soothes you when you are ill? Who refuses to leave you when you are impoverished and stretches its resources to give a hearty sustenance and cheer? Who warms you in the winter and cools you in the summer? Yet who also is capable of doing honor to your richest table and impressing your most demanding guests? Soup does its loyal best, no matter what undignified conditions are imposed upon it. You don't catch steak hanging around when you're poor and sick, do you?"

-*Judith Martin (Miss Manners)*

# charleston she-crab soup

*This award-winning recipe comes from 82 Queen, the premier restaurant in Charleston. This serves 12 and can be easily halved to serve 6. If crab roe is not available, you can get similar results by using hard-boiled egg yolks, crumbling about two tablespoons in the bottom of each bowl.*

1 pound crabmeat (divided in half)
$^1/_2$ pound of crab roe (divided in half)
2 tablespoons butter
1 cup chopped celery
$^1/_4$ cup chopped onion
$^1/_4$ cup chopped carrots
$^1/_2$ cup butter
$^1/_2$ cup flour
3 cups whole milk
1 cup heavy cream
2 cups fish stock, or a mixture of water and fish stock*
$^1/_4$ cup sherry wine
1 tablespoon Tabasco® sauce
1 tablespoon Worcestershire sauce
4 tablespoons minced chives or minced parsley (garnish)

**1.** Melt 2 tablespoons butter in a medium skillet over medium-low heat, until the butter begins to foam (be careful not to burn it). Add the celery, onions and carrots. Sauté the vegetables until they are soft and translucent. Set aside.

**2.** In a large soup pot, melt $^1/_2$ cup butter, add the flour, and then stir constantly until the roux is golden and smooth. Add milk and cream. Bring to slow boil, stirring constantly. Add the fish stock, wine, Tabasco® sauce, Worcestershire sauce, half of the crabmeat, and half of the crab roe. Simmer the soup for 20 minutes.

**3.** Ladle the soup into bowls. Add the remaining half of the crabmeat to the center of each bowl, and sprinkle the remaining half of the crab roe around the crabmeat. Garnish with chives or parsley.

***\*Claim juice or chicken broth may also be substituted for fish stock.***

*Serves 12*

# cajun crab & shrimp gumbo

*Gumbo is a New Orleans signature dish. The key to a great gumbo is the roux, which requires a slow cooking process until the roux is a deep chocolate brown. Although a good roux can take as long as 30 minutes to make, it is well worth the effort. You'll be rewarded with a rich, delicious gumbo.*

$^1/_4$ cup vegetable oil
6 tablespoon flour
2 cups chopped onion
1 cup chopped celery
1 cup chopped green pepper
1 teaspoon dried oregano leaves
1 teaspoon dried thyme leaves
2 bay leaves
2 cloves garlic, minced
8 cups chicken stock or chicken broth, warmed
3 cups water
$^1/_2$ teaspoon ground cayenne pepper
1 tablespoon Worcestershire sauce
1 teaspoon salt
$^1/_2$ teaspoon black pepper
1 (10-ounce) can diced tomatoes with green chiles
1 (8-ounce) can tomato sauce
1 tablespoon sugar
2 teaspoons Zatarain's® Crab Boil seasoning
1 pound small or medium shrimp, peeled
$^3/_4$ pound crabmeat (lump meat works great)
1 tablespoon filé powder* (optional)
cooked rice (if desired)

**1.** To make the roux, heat the oil in a large stockpot over medium heat. Gradually whisk in the flour and cook, whisking constantly, until the roux is a dark chocolate color.

**2.** Add the onion, celery, pepper, oregano, thyme, and bay leaves, stirring constantly. You may want to lower the heat, once the onions are transparent. Add the garlic, cook another minute, slowly add the chicken stock (or chicken broth), and continue stirring. Next, add the water, cayenne pepper, Worcestershire sauce, salt, pepper, diced tomatoes, tomato sauce, sugar, and Zatarain's® Crab Boil seasoning.

**3.** Cover the pot and simmer the liquid for 1 to 1$^{1}/_{2}$ hours, stirring occasionally. Add the shrimp, let it simmer for 15 minutes, and then stir in the crabmeat. Remove the pot from the heat.

**4.** Mix the filé powder with $^{1}/_{4}$ cup of water, and then add it to the gumbo.

**5.** Serve the gumbo over rice, if you like.

*Note: Filé Powder (FEE-lay) is used as a seasoning and thickener, made from the ground dried leaves of sassafras trees. Filé powder has a wonderfully pungent and aromatic flavor. It must be stirred in after the cooking is done, because it becomes tough and stringy when it is heated. If you think you'll have leftover gumbo, filé can be added to each bowl individually. Filé powder can be found in the spice section at the market.*

I use the filé powder instead of okra to thicken the gumbo. If you like okra, by all means add it (1 cup, trimmed and cut into 1-inch pieces).

*Serves 4-6*

"Somewhere lives a bad Cajun cook, just as somewhere must live one ivory-billed woodpecker. For me, I don't expect ever to encounter either one."
     *-William Least Heat Moon, Blue Highways, 1982*

# cognac-laced crab bisque

*Crab bisque is a truly timeless, elegant soup. This velvety smooth version will bring you rave reviews.*

4 tablespoons butter
$1/3$ cup shallots
2 cloves garlic, minced
2 tablespoons flour
2 cups chicken stock (or chicken broth) or dry white wine
1 cup whipping cream
2 tablespoons tomato paste (preferably the tubed variety)
1 bay leaf
1 teaspoon dried tarragon
1 teaspoon salt
$1/8$ teaspoon ground cayenne pepper
$1/2$ teaspoon white pepper
$1/4$ cup cognac
2 cups crabmeat

2 tablespoon minced parsley (garnish)
dash of paprika (garnish)

**1.** Melt the butter in a large saucepan over medium-low heat until it foams. Add the shallots, cover the pan, and reduce the heat to low. Cook for 3 minutes, add the garlic, and cook for about 2 more minutes. Whisk in the flour and continue cooking, stirring for about 3 minutes. Slowly whisk in the chicken stock (or broth or wine) and whipping cream. Next, add the tomato paste, bay leaf, tarragon, salt and cayenne pepper.

**2.** Return the soup to medium-high heat, and stir it until it boils. Reduce the heat and simmer, stirring occasionally, for about 10 minutes. Add the white pepper, cognac and crabmeat. Cook for 10 more minutes.

**3.** Serve in heated bowls. Garnish with parsley and a sprinkle of paprika.

*Serves 4-6*

# dungeness crab,
# red potato and corn chowder

*Chowder is the ultimate comfort food, so warm and soothing. Serve this soup with some hot crusty rolls and a green salad for a winning combination.*

5 slices bacon, chopped
2 tablespoons butter
1 cup chopped onion
$^1/_2$ cup chopped red pepper
1 fresh jalapeno pepper, minced (optional)
4 medium ears sweet corn, shucked (about 2 cups)*
3 tablespoons flour
4 cups chicken stock
1 teaspoon salt
$^3/_4$ teaspoon freshly ground black pepper
$1^1/_2$ cup red potatoes, cut into $^1/_2$-inch dice
1 cup heavy cream
$^3/_4$ cup crabmeat
fresh minced chives (garnish)

**1.** Cook the bacon in a large soup pot over low heat, until fat is rendered.

**2.** Add the butter, onions and red pepper, and then sauté until they are soft (about 8 minutes). Stir in the jalapeno pepper (if using) and corn, sautéing them another 2 to 3 minutes. Stir in the flour until well incorporated, and continue cooking about 5 minutes. Add the chicken stock, salt and black pepper.

**3.** Bring the soup to a boil, lower the heat, and add the potatoes. Let the soup simmer for about 15 to 20 minutes, until potatoes are tender.

**4.** Stir in the cream and crabmeat, cooking for another 5 minutes, and then the chowder is ready to serve! Ladle into bowls and sprinkle with chives.

If you reheat the chowder, do so over low heat, being careful to not let it boil.

*** Frozen corn may be used instead.**

# santa fe gazpacho

*Cool and refreshing on a hot summer day, this gazpacho has just the right amount of kick. And best of all, there's no cooking required. This is my rendition of the seafood gazpacho found in The Silver Palate cookbook by Julee Rosso and Sheila Lunkins, one of my all-time favorite cookbooks. It is best to make this soup with really ripe, vine-ripened tomatoes.*

5 vine-ripened tomatoes, cored and cut into $^1/_4$-inch dice
2 red bell peppers, cut into $^1/_4$-inch dice
$^1/_2$ yellow bell pepper, cut into $^1/_4$-inch dice
3 jalapeno peppers, stemmed, cored and seeded
$^1/_2$ cup red onion, finely chopped
1 cucumber peeled, seeded and cut into $^1/_4$-inch dice
1 cup minced cilantro leaves (reserve 2 tablespoons for garnish)
5 cups tomato juice or vegetable juice
$^1/_4$ cup lime juice
$^1/_3$ cup light olive oil
1 tablespoon sugar
1 $^1/_2$ teaspoons salt
$^3/_4$ teaspoon freshly ground black pepper
2 cups fresh bread crumbs
2 cloves of garlic, minced
1 pound of crabmeat (reserve $^1/_3$ cup for garnish)
1 avocado

**1.** Combine the tomatoes, bell peppers, jalapeno peppers, onion, cucumber and cilantro in  a large bowl. Pour in the tomato juice (or vegetable juice), lime juice, oil, sugar, salt, and pepper. Combine the bread crumbs and garlic, and then add it to the tomato mixture.

**2.** Puree half the soup in blender or food processor. Combine the puree with the unpureed portion of the soup. Add the crabmeat and chill the soup for at least 3 hours, or overnight.

**To Serve:**
Peel and cut the avocado into ¼-inch dice, and then stir into the soup. Ladle soup into bowls and place a small mound of reserved crab in the middle of each bowl. Sprinkle the reserved cilantro on top of the crabmeat.

*Note: Instead of adding most of the crabmeat to the soup, another variation is using all the crabmeat to mound in the middle of soup bowls . Using roasted red bell peppers instead of fresh ones add another dimension of flavor.*

*Serves 4*

**Avocados**
To speed the ripening process,
place avocados in a flour filled paper bag,
and store at room temperature
until ready to eat.

# brazilian crab soup

*Crab plays an important role in Brazilian cuisine. There are two types of crab in Brazil: sira (a saltwater crab similar to the blue crab) and caranguejo or land crab (which is found in rivers). This delicious soup can be made in about 20 minutes.*

2 tablespoons butter
1 cup of finely chopped onion
2 cloves garlic, minced
2 serrano chiles, stemmed, seeded and minced
1 tablespoon flour
3 cups chicken stock or chicken broth
$1/2$ cup half-and-half or unsweetened coconut milk
$1/2$ teaspoon salt
$1/4$ teaspoon freshly ground black pepper
$1/4$ teaspoon ground cayenne pepper
$1/2$ pound of crabmeat
2 tablespoons chopped cilantro

**1.** Melt the butter in a large saucepan over medium-low heat. Sauté the onion until soft, and then add the garlic and chiles, sautéing for another 2 minutes. Add the flour, and stir for another minute, until well-combined. Add the chicken stock (or chicken broth) & half-and-half (or coconut milk), salt, pepper and cayenne pepper.

**2.** Bring to a boil, turn heat to low, and simmer for 10 minutes.

**3.** Add the crabmeat and cilantro. Cook for 5 more minutes.

*Serves 2-3*

# thai coconut crab soup

*The soup created by reknowned Chef Joey Altman captured top honors at the "Challenge of the Masters" cooking competition during the 2003 San Francisco Crab and Wine Festival.*

**Soup:**
2 tablespoons extra virgin olive oil
4 tablespoons chopped shallots
2 teaspoons minced ginger
2 teaspoons minced garlic
2 (14-ounce) cans coconut milk
2 cups chicken stock
1/2 cup fresh lime juice
2 tablespoons fish sauce
2 tablespoons sambal oelek (chili sauce)
2 tablespoons chopped cilantro

**Crab Mix:**
1 tablespoon extra virgin olive oil
4 scallions, minced
12 ounces fresh Dungeness crabmeat
salt
freshly ground black pepper
4 fresh cilantro sprigs (garnish)

**1.** Place a heavy-bottomed 4-quart sauce pot on medium heat. Add 2 tablespoons of the olive oil, the shallots, ginger and garlic, and sir frequently for 2 minutes or until the shallots are tender. Add the coconut milk and chicken stock. Reduce the heat to low and simmer for 10 minutes.

**2.** In a small skillet on high heat, add 1 tablespoon of olive oil, sauté the scallions for 1 minute, and then transfer them to a small mixing bowl. Mix the scallions with the crabmeat and season to taste with salt and pepper.

**3.** Add the lime juice, fish sauce and sambal oelek to the soup, and season to taste. Divide the soup into 4 bowls and top each one with 1/4 of the crab mix. Garnish with cilantro sprigs and serve immediately.

*Serves 4*

# main dishes & entrees

# MAIN DISHES & ENTREES

beer battered soft-shell crab

chesapeake bay steamed blue crab

chili crab with garlic noodles

citrus grilled soft-shell crab

garlic roasted dungeness crab

crab au gratin in scallop shells

creamy crab enchiladas

crab ravioli with roasted red pepper sauce

crab cakes with roasted corn salsa

grilled marinated dungeness crab

king crab with garlic butter & roasted rosemary potatoes

louisiana crab boil

san francisco cioppino

paupiette de saumon au crabe

mendo bistro's award-winning crab cakes

macadamia-crusted crab cakes with mango salsa

sautéed soft-shell crab with wine, lemon & caper pan sauce

soft shell crab in tempura batter with ponzu dipping sauce

spanish crab & artichoke paella

# beer battered soft-shell crab

*One of my all-time favorites. Cole slaw and sliced tomatoes are traditional accompaniments.*

1 cup flour
$1/2$ teaspoon salt
$1/2$ teaspoon garlic powder
$1/2$ teaspoon baking powder
$1/4$ teaspoon ground cayenne pepper
1 cup dark beer

12 soft-shell crab

flour for dusting
vegetable oil for frying

**1.** Sift together flour, salt, garlic powder, baking powder and cayenne in a large bowl. Whisk in beer. Let the mixture sit at room temperate for at least 1 hour. This allows the batter to thicken.

**2.** Preheat the oven to 225°. Blot crab with paper towels to remove any excess moisture. Lightly dust crab with flour, shaking off excess.

**3.** Heat about 3 inches of oil to 360° in a large heavy skillet. Dip the crab, 2 to 3 at a time, in the beer batter, then carefully place in skillet. Fry until golden brown, about 3 to 5 minutes. Turning once, remove the crab and place them on a paper-toweled baking sheet. Place in a warm oven while preparing remaining crab.

*Serves 4-6 (Depending on size of crab)*

# chesapeake bay steamed blue crab

*A true Chesapeake Bay tradition. Allow at least 4 to 6 crabs per person depending on size of the crab and your friends! Serve with lots of napkins or paper towels. This is messy!*

3 cups beer (or water)
3 cups white vinegar
2 dozen live blue hard crabs
$^1/_2$ cup salt
$^1/_2$ cup Old Bay® Seasoning
melted butter

**1.** Place a rack in the bottom of a large, non-reactive pot. The rack should be at least 2 inches off the bottom of the pot. Pour in the beer and vinegar, which should stay just below the level of the rack.

**2.** Place about 6 crabs on the rack and sprinkle with 3 tablespoons of Old Bay® Seasoning. Add another 6 crabs, sprinkle with another 2 to 3 tablespoons of Old Bay® Seasoning, and continue until all of the crabs and the seasoning are in the pot.

**3.** Heat the liquid to a boil, cover, reduce heat to a simmer, and steam, until the crabs turn red, about 20 to 25 minutes.

**4.** Transfer to large platters and serve hot with melted butter.

# chili crab with garlic noodles

*This is messy, but oh so good!*

**Garlic Noodles:**

12 ounces (fresh or dried) Chinese medium egg noodles

2 tablespoons olive oil

3 tablespoons chopped garlic

2 tablespoons sesame oil

2 tablespoons soy sauce

$1/2$ tablespoon sugar

$1/2$ teaspoon dried chili flakes

$1/2$ cup thinly sliced scallions

2 tablespoons chopped cilantro (garnish)

**Chili Crab:**

3 tablespoons  oil

3 garlic cloves, minced

1 shallot, minced

1 (2-inch) piece fresh ginger, minced

2 teaspoons dark soy sauce

1 teaspoons salt

$1/2$ teaspoon freshly ground black pepper

2 teaspoons sugar

6 fresh red chilies, stemmed, seeded and chopped (or dried red chilies, soaked in water and chopped)

2 scallions, chopped

1 live or pre-cooked Dungeness crab, cleaned, or 4 live or pre-cooked blue crab, cleaned

$1/4$ cup sherry

$1/4$ cup chicken broth

1 teaspoon cornstarch, dissolved in $1/4$ cup water

*Prepare the Garlic Noodles:*

**1.** Bring a large pot of water to a rolling boil. Stir in the noodles. Cook until just done: 4 minutes for fresh and 10 minutes for dried. Remove them from the heat, rinse in cool water and drain completely.

**2.** Heat the oil in a large skillet over medium heat. Add the garlic, and stir until fragrant and golden (not brown), for about 20 seconds. Add the sesame oil, soy sauce, sugar, chili flakes and the scallions. Add the noodles and evenly coat them with the sauce. Transfer to a serving platter. Place in warm oven, while the crab is being prepared.

***Prepare the Chili Crab:***
**1.** Clean the crab and separate claws from body. Crack the claws and legs, and cut the body into 4 to 6 pieces.

**2.** Heat the oil in a large wok or skillet over medium heat. Add the garlic, shallot and ginger and quickly stir-fry until golden (about 10 seconds). Add the soy sauce, salt, pepper, sugar, chilies, scallions and crab. Stir-fry until shells begin to turn red. Add sherry and chicken broth. Cover and let simmer for 7 minutes. Remove cover and stir in cornstarch. Stir until saucy, about 2 to 3 minutes.

***To Serve:***
Transfer the crab to the platter containing the garlic noodles and arrange on top. Garnish with the cilantro and serve immediately with lots of napkins. Yum Yum!

*Serves 2 generously*

"My doctor told me to stop having intimate dinners for four. Unless there are three other people."

*-Orson Welles*

# citrus grilled soft-shell crab

*Prepare the marinade ahead of time to allow the flavors to meld.*
*Marinate 1 hour, prior to grilling.*

2/3 cup fresh lime juice
½ cup olive oil
2 cloves garlic, minced
¼ cup chopped cilantro
1 jalapeno pepper, stemmed, seeded and minced
½ teaspoon salt
¼ teaspoon freshly ground black pepper
12 soft-shell crab

**1.** Combine the lime juice, oil, garlic, cilantro, pepper, salt and pepper in a small bowl, and whisk to blend. Place the crab in a shallow bowl and cover with the marinade. Refrigerate for 1 hour, prior to grilling.

**2.** Prepare a medium-hot charcoal grill or pre-heat a gas grill to medium-high. When the grill is ready, remove the crab from marinade and grill them 3 to 4 inches from the heat. Grill 3 to 4 minutes on each side.

*Serves 4*

### Cilantro

I've often been disappointed when a day or two after buying cilantro, it's so wilted that it's unusable. I found that placing it in a large cup of water with the stems completely submerged up to the leaves. It will last a week or longer.

# garlic roasted dungeness crab

*This is my family's favorite and my most requested dish. I've yet to come across anyone who hasn't loved this. The roasting makes the crab shell brittle, making it even easier to get the crabmeat out of the shell. I serve this with steamed potatoes, salad, some good bread and white wine. The recipe comes from Bonnie McCullough, the innkeeper at the Selah Inn in Belfair, Washington.*

$^1$/$_3$ cup butter
$^1$/$_3$ cup olive oil
3 tablespoons minced garlic
4 Dungeness crab, cleaned, cooked and cracked
1 teaspoon salt
$^1$/$_2$ teaspoon freshly ground black pepper
3 tablespoons fresh lemon juice
$^1$/$_4$ cup chopped fresh parsley
lemon slices (garnish)

**1.** Preheat the oven to 500 ° .

**2.** Heat the butter, oil and garlic in a large saucepan over medium-high heat. Sauté for 3 to 4 minutes. Add the crab, toss the mixture well, and season to taste with salt and pepper. Transfer the crab mixture to a large baking pan.

**3.** Place the roasting pan in the preheated oven and cook for 10 to 15 minutes. Oven temperatures vary, so watch the pan closely, making sure the crab mixture doesn't burn. It should be heated completely through and the sauce should be braised onto the shell.

**4.** Remove the dish from the oven. Sprinkle lemon juice and chopped parsley over the top, and toss to combine. Transfer to a serving platter. Garnish with lemon slices and serve immediately.

*Serves 4*

"As for butter versus margarine,
I trust cows more than chemists"
-Joan Dye Gussowg

# crab au gratin in scallop shells

*A romantic dinner for two served in scallop shells (sold in gourmet or shell shops).*
*Ramekins may be substituted for the scallop shells. A combination of crab and*
*shrimp may also be used. Make adjustments accordingly.*

3 tablespoons butter
$^3/_4$ cup chopped onions
$^1/_4$ cup chopped red bell pepper
$^3/_4$ cup minced scallions
1 clove garlic, minced
$^1/_4$ cup minced flat-leaf parsley
1 cup dry bread crumbs (reserve $^1/_4$ cup for topping)
$^1/_2$ teaspoon salt
$^1/_4$ teaspoon black pepper
$^1/_4$ teaspoon ground cayenne pepper
1 egg, beaten
$^1/_2$ cup vermouth
1 teaspoon fresh lemon juice
$1^1/_2$ teaspoon grated lemon zest
8 ounces crabmeat
1 tablespoon butter
$^1/_4$ cup finely grated Parmesan cheese (for topping)

Preheat the oven to 350°

### Prepare crab mixture:
**1.** Melt the butter in a medium skillet over medium-low heat, and then add onions, red bell pepper, scallions and garlic. Sauté until softened, about 5 to 7 minutes, stirring occasionally. Add parsley, and cook 1 more minute. Remove from heat. medium bowl.

**2.** In a medium bowl, mix the bread crumbs, salt, pepper and cayenne pepper. Add the beaten egg, vermouth, lemon juice and zest. Gently fold in the crabmeat.

***To Assemble:***

**1.** Butter the scallop shells or ramekins.

**2.** In a small bowl, combine ¼ cup bread crumbs and Parmesan cheese. Divide crab mixture evenly into shells. Top the crab mixture with the bread crumb mixture, and dot the tops with butter.

**3.** Bake for 12 minutes. Turn on broiler and broil until the top is bubbly and golden brown. Serve immediately.

*Serves 2*

"Cooking is like love. It should be entered into with abandon or not at all."
-Harriet Van Horne, VOGUE, October 15, 1956

# creamy crab enchiladas

*I don't think I've ever had better enchiladas. Though a lot of work, they're worth it! While I'm generally not a fan of chain restaurants, Chevy's is the exception. These enchiladas are my rendition of the ones served at the restaurant. I serve these with black beans and a salad with citrus dressing. These can be assembled ahead of time and refrigerated until you are ready to bake.*

1 pound of crabmeat

**For the sauce:**
4 tablespoons butter
1 tablespoon oil
1 cup onion, chopped
$^1/_2$ cup minced red bell pepper
1 jalapeno pepper, stemmed, seeded and minced
1 cup chopped scallions (white and green parts)
1 (8-ounce) package cream cheese
1 cup heavy cream
2 tablespoons fresh lime juice
1 teaspoon garlic powder
$^1/_4$ cup minced cilantro
2 canned Chipotle peppers in adobe sauce, finely chopped (about 1 tablespoon)
pinch of sugar
1 teaspoon salt
$^1/_2$ teaspoon freshly ground black pepper
1 cup Monterey Jack cheese or Pepper Jack cheese
Oil
8 to 12 white corn tortillas
1 ½ cups queso fresco* crumbled

*Prepare sauce:*
**1.** Heat the butter and oil in a small pan over medium-high heat. Once butter has melted, add the onion and sauté until translucent. Add the red bell pepper, jalapeno pepper, and scallions. Sauté about 1 minute until just soft.

**2.** Decrease the heat to low, adding cream cheese, heavy cream, lime juice, garlic powder, cilantro, chipotle peppers, sugar, salt and pepper. Simmer for 7 to10 minutes.

**3.** Remove the saucepan from heat and stir in the cheese. Keep the sauce warm.

*Prepare tortillas:*
Heat a small amount of oil in a medium pan, just enough to coat the pan, over medium heat. Place the tortillas in the pan, one at a time, and heat both sides until softened. Stack the heated tortillas and set aside.

*Prepare crab filling:*
Gently fold in ¾ cup of the sauce into the crabmeat in a medium bowl.

*Assembly:*
**1.** Preheat the oven to 375°.

**2.** In a 9x13-inch baking pan, spread 3 tablespoons of the sauce on the bottom, just enough to barely cover the surface.

**3.** Set a tortilla on your work surface and place about ⅓ cup of crab filling down the center of the tortilla. Roll it tightly. Transfer the rolled enchilada, seam-side down, to the baking pan. Repeat this process for each tortilla.

**4.** Pour the remaining sauce over the enchiladas. Sprinkle cheese over the top. Bake the enchiladas for 20 minutes. Serve  with salsa fresca, page 118.

*\* Queso fresco is a mild flavored, crumbly white Mexican cheese. It's available in well-stocked grocery stores or Hispanic markets. It freezes well and can be frozen for up to 3 months. A mild feta cheese may be substituted.*

*Serves 6*

# crab ravioli with roasted red pepper sauce

*Always a favorite. Instead of pasta, this ravioli is made with wonton wrappers.*

**For the Ravioli:**
2 tablespoons butter
2 tablespoons olive oil
$1/2$ cup chopped scallions
1 tablespoon finely minced red pepper
2 cups crabmeat
zest of $1/2$ lemon
salt
freshly ground black pepper
$1/2$ cup ricotta cheese
$1/4$ cup crème fraîche (sour cream may be substituted)
$1/8$ teaspoon ground cayenne pepper
2 tablespoons fresh lemon juice
1 teaspoon garlic powder
4 tablespoons finely chopped fresh basil (divided)
1 package wonton wrappers
1 egg white, beaten

**Roasted Red Pepper Sauce**
2 tablespoons butter
1 shallot, finely chopped
2 cloves garlic, finely chopped
4 roasted red peppers*
1 cup white wine
1 cup chicken broth
1 cup heavy cream

*Prepare the ravioli filling:*
**1.** Heat the butter and oil over medium-low heat in a large frying pan. Add scallions and red pepper, and turn up heat to medium. Sauté the vegetables until softened. Add the crabmeat

and cook until heated, about 1 minute. Add the lemon zest, and then salt and pepper to taste. Remove crabmeat mixture from heat.

**2.** In a large bowl, add the ricotta, crème fraíche, cayenne pepper, lemon juice, garlic powder and 2 ½ tablespoons of the basil. Season to taste with salt and pepper. Mix well. Next add the crabmeat mixture. Cover and refrigerate the filling for at least 1 hour, up to 24 hours.

*Assemble the ravioli:*
**1.** On a lightly floured surface, lay the won ton wrappers side by side.

**2.** Spoon 1 tablespoon of the crab filling into the center of each won ton wrapper, and then lightly brush the edges (using a small basting brush) with the beaten egg white.

**3.** Cover each one with another won ton wrapper, pressing out any air pockets to seal. With the tines of a fork, press the edges down. Transfer the ravioli to a baking sheet, cover them with a kitchen towel, and refrigerate if not using immediately.

*Prepare the sauce:*
**1.** Sauté the shallots in butter for about 3 minutes. Add garlic and roasted peppers, sautéing for about 3 more minutes. Add wine and cook until reduced by half. Add broth and reduce by half, and then add cream, once again reducing by half (be careful not to boil the sauce).

**2.** Transfer the sauce to a blender and puree until smooth.

**3.** Return the pureed sauce to low heat and whisk in the butter. Season to taste with salt and pepper.

*Final preparation:*
**1.** Place ravioli in simmering water (do not boil to avoid damaging delicate ravioli). When they float to the surface, cook an additional 3 minutes.

**2.** Transfer the ravioli to warmed plates with a slotted spoon. Spoon the sauce on top. Garnish with the remaining basil. Enjoy!

*Serves 6*

*\*Char bell peppers over gas flame or in broiler until blackened on all sides. Enclose in plastic bag 10 minutes. Peel, seed, and coarsely chop bell peppers. Roasted red bell peppers from a jar may also be used.*

# chilled cracked crab with
# 3 dipping sauces

*This is a great meal for entertaining. Everything can be prepared and assembled ahead of time. Serve with a tossed salad, some good bread and wine and you've got a fabulous meal. There are two ways you can serve the crab, one way is to serve crab on a large platter, the other is to place one crab on each plate. If this is your preference, save the shells for the presentation. If you purchase your crab cooked, have your fishmonger clean it and ask for the shells back. This "special sauce" comes from my good friend and one of the best cooks I know Kelly MacDonald. It's been in her family 30 years. When you taste it you'll know why.*

6 Dungeness crab live or cooked crab in the shell
$^1/_4$  cup salt for cooking water
Lemon wedges

**Kelly's Special Sauce**
1 cup mayonnaise (Best Foods)
$^1/_2$ cup ketchup
1 $^1/_2$ teaspoons Worcestershire sauce
$^1/_8$ teaspoon cayenne
$^1/_8$ teaspoon granulated garlic
$^1/_4$  teaspoon black pepper
$^1/_8$  teaspoon McCormick's salad supreme seasoning
$^1/_8$ cup red wine vinegar
In a small bowl, whisk mayonnaise until smooth to eliminate lumps. Add ketchup stir well and add remaining ingredients mixing well. Refrigerate until ready to use.

**Lemon Aioli***
2 egg yolks at room temperature
$^1/_4$ cup fresh squeezed lemon juice
1 tablespoon grated lemon zest
2 small cloves garlic minced**
$^1/_2$ teaspoon salt
$^1/_8$ teaspoon white pepper
$^1/_8$ teaspoon cayenne
1 teaspoon Dijon mustard
$^1/_2$  teaspoon sugar

2 cups oil (I like to use 1 cup of olive and 1 cup canola)

In a blender or food processor, combine egg yolks, lemon juice, zest, garlic, salt, white pepper, cayenne, mustard, & sugar. Blend or process about 10 seconds, With blender running slowly add oil in a slow stream blending until an emulsion forms. Stop blending or processing once all the oil has been added. Taste and adjust seasoning if needed. Refrigerate until ready to use.

## Spicy Cocktail Sauce

2 cups ketchup

1 $1/2$ tablespoons prepared horseradish

2 tablespoons Worcestershire sauce

1 tablespoon fresh lemon juice

1 teaspoon black pepper

Combine all ingredients in a small bowl, stirring well. Refrigerate until ready to use.

## Cook Crab:

If using live crab, otherwise proceed to serving, if using cooked. You may need to use two pots or cook crab in two batches. One way to eliminating the need for two pots or cooking in batches is to clean the crab first (see cleaning crab).

Bring large pot of salted water to a boil, plunge crab in, when water returns to a boil cook 18- 20 minutes. The shells will turn bright red. Remove crab with tongs and immerse in ice-water to stop the cooking process, cool 10-15 minutes. I fill one side of my sink up with cold water and lots of ice. Once cooled, clean crab
if not already done. Refrigerate until ready to serve.

## To Serve:

If serving on a platter, arrange crab on large platter, scatter lemon wedges around platter. For individual servings, place one crab on each plate, top crab with shell, and garnish with lemon wedges.

Place a large bowl on the table for crab shells.

*Serves 6*

*\* For a quicker version of the lemon aioli. Combine 2 cups of mayonnaise with lemon juice, lemon zest, cayenne and Dijon mustard. Typically aioli contains more garlic than I included in this recipe. I wanted to let all the lemon flavors shine through. If you're so inclined add 3-5 additional cloves of garlic.*

# crab cakes with roasted corn salsa

*This is one of my all-time favorite crab cakes. The secret ingredient is potatoes. I was originally skeptical about the idea of using potatoes, seeing the potatoes simply as a filler, but I can't resist a new crab cake recipe and have to try each one I come across. What a revelation! People are always surprised when they find out that these are made with potatoes, because they are absolutely delicious. They're a great way to stretch the amount of crab on hand. But that's not the only reason to make these tasty crab cakes. You don't need to refrigerate these crab cakes prior to cooking, as they hold their shape quite well. You'll also love the flavors in the roasted corn salsa—the perfect accompaniment to these crab cakes.*

**Roasted Corn Salsa:**
1 cup of roasted corn kernels (1 to 2 ears)
2 tablespoons olive oil
1/4 cup chopped scallions
1/4 cup chopped red bell pepper
3 tablespoons chopped fresh cilantro
2 tablespoons fresh lime juice
2 plum tomatoes, finely chopped
2 jalapeno peppers, stemmed, seeded and minced
1/2 teaspoon salt
1/4 teaspoon freshly ground black pepper

**Crab Cakes:**
3/4 pound russet potatoes (about 2 medium)
1 tablespoon butter
1/3 cup minced red bell pepper
1/3 cup minced scallions (white and green parts)
1 tablespoon minced garlic
1 tablespoon minced jalapeno peppers
1/4 cup mayonnaise
1 egg, beaten
2 teaspoons salt
1/2 teaspoon freshly ground black pepper
1/4 teaspoon ground cayenne pepper
1 pound crabmeat, excess moisture squeezed out
1/4 cup dry bread crumbs
3 tablespoons butter
3 tablespoons canola oil

### Prepare the Salsa:

**1.** Preheat oven or prepare grill to medium heat. Husk the corn, and baste with olive oil.

**2.** Grill or broil the corn 4 inches from the heat until they are golden, about 10 minutes.

**3.** Scrape kernels into a medium bowl, and stir in scallions, bell pepper, cilantro, lime juice, tomatoes and jalapeno peppers. Season to taste with salt and pepper.

**4.** Refrigerate the salsa for at least one hour prior to serving. Serve cold or at room temperature.

### Prepare the Crab Cakes:

**1.** Preheat oven to 375° . Bake the potatoes, until they're easily pierced with a fork. Remove their skin and grate them, using the largest holes of a grater (the one you grate cheese on), until you have 2 cups. Do not pack the potatoes down.

**2.** Heat 1 tablespoon of butter in a small skillet, over medium-low heat. Add red pepper, scallions, garlic and jalapeno pepper, and cook them until soft (about 2-4 minutes). Set aside.*

**3.** In a large bowl, whisk mayonnaise, egg, vegetable mixture, salt, pepper and cayenne pepper. Gently fold in crab, potatoes and bread crumbs with a spatula, and mix them gently just to combine. Shape into 6 cakes about 3 inches wide.

**4.** Heat butter and oil over medium-low heat in a large skillet. Add crab cakes and cook, turning once, until golden brown, about 5-7 minutes on each side. Serve hot with corn salsa on the side.

***If you prefer, this step can be skipped and you can use the fresh red pepper, scallions, garlic and jalapeno without sautéing.***

*Serves 4*

# grilled marinated dungeness crab

*Grilled crab is an unbeatable treat. Grilling intensifies the succulent flavors of crab.*
*The dry heat of the grill makes the shell brittle, making it easy to crack.*

4 cleaned Dungeness crab (live or pre-cooked)

**For the marinade:**
1 cup extra virgin olive oil
$^1/_4$ cup white wine vinegar
4 cloves garlic, minced
2 tablespoons fresh lemon juice
1 teaspoon sugar
1 teaspoon salt
$^1/_2$ teaspoon freshly ground black pepper
$^1/_2$ teaspoon dried, crushed red pepper
$^1/_4$ cup flat-leaf parsley, chopped
$^1/_2$ teaspoon dried basil, crumbled
pinch of dried oregano

*Prepare the marinade:*
**1.** Combine oil, vinegar, garlic, lemon juice, sugar, salt, black pepper, red pepper, parsley, basil and oregano in a small bowl, and whisk to blend.

**2.** If using live crab, bring a large pot of salted water to a boil, drop the crab in, and cook for exactly 5 minutes. Remove the crab from heat, and plunge it into ice water to stop the cooking process. Clean and crack the crab.

**3.** Place the crab in a shallow bowl and cover with the marinade. Refrigerate for at least 1 hour or up to 6 hours.

*To grill:*
Prepare a medium-hot charcoal grill or preheat a gas grill to medium. Basting every few minutes, grill each side for 5-8 minutes with cover on, if previously cooked. Grill 8-10 minutes each side if you are using live crab, Serve immediately.

*Serves 4*

# king crab with garlic butter
# & roasted rosemary potatoes

*This is a truly luxurious and memorable meal. Serve it with a tossed green salad and garlic bread.*

2 $^1/_2$ pounds red potatoes, cut in half
3 tablespoons extra virgin olive oil
4 cloves garlic, minced (2 for garlic butter, 2 for potatoes)
2 tablespoons fresh rosemary, chopped
1 teaspoon salt
1 teaspoon freshly ground black pepper
1 cup melted butter (2 sticks)
$^1/_4$ cup minced flat-leaf parsley
lemon wedges for serving
4 pounds king crab legs, split

**Roasted Potatoes:**
**1.** Preheat the oven to 400°. Preheat a shallow roasting pan or baking sheet (this will help keep the potatoes from sticking).

**2.** In a large bowl, toss potatoes with olive oil, garlic, rosemary, salt and pepper. Place the potatoes flesh-side down on the preheated pan or baking sheet. Cover tightly with aluminum foil and cook about 25 minutes.

**3.** While the potatoes are roasting, add the remaining garlic to the melted butter. Remove the foil and stir potatoes, cooking 15 minutes more or until they're tender when pierced with a fork. Once done, sprinkle all but 2 tablespoons of the parsley over the potatoes. Cover the potatoes and keep them warm, while the crab is prepared.

**King Crab Legs:**
Turn on the broiler. Brush the crab legs with garlic butter, reserving the remainder for the dipping sauce. Broil the crab legs close to the heat source for 6 to 7 minutes. Be careful not to overcook them.

**To Serve:**
Transfer the crab legs to a large platter and arrange the potatoes around them. Sprinkle the remaining parsley over the crab legs. Serve with the garlic butter (in butter warmers or individual ramekins) and lemon wedges. Enjoy!

*Serves 4*

# Old Bay Seasoning

The granddaddy of all seafood herb-and-spice blends—began its claim to fame more than 60 years ago when German immigrant Gustav Brunn, with a suitcase in one hand  and grinder in the other, arrived in the U.S. and settled in Baltimore on the Chesapeake Bay. Determined to start a business Brunn and his wife, armed with a secret recipe called Delicious Brand Seafood Seasoning, set up shop across from the busy Wholesale Fish Market. Although business was brisk, one look around was all it took for Brunn to see his future: crabs. Calling on his 20 years of experience at spice making, he went to work concocting a secret blend of more than a dozen herbs and spices, including celery salt, bay leaf, mustard, red pepper, and ginger. All that was missing was a name. After some deliberation while sitting on the Baltimore docks, he christened his product after the steamship line Old Bay that traveled the Chesapeake from Maryland to Virginia. McCormick & Co. purchased Old Bay in 1990.

# louisiana crab boil

*What could be more fun? Serve on newspaper and with paper plates. When everyone's done eating and all the silverware's accounted for, simply roll it all up and throw it away.*

3 bottles lager beer
2 (3-ounce) packets Zatarain's® Crab Boil seasoning
$^1/_2$ cup salt
3 pounds small new potatoes
18 to 24 live Blue crab
3 pounds crayfish (optional)
6 to 8 ears of corn, husked and cut in half
2 pounds medium-to-large shrimp with shell
3 pounds spicy sausage, cut into 2- to 3-inch pieces
$^1/_4$ cup Old Bay® Seasoning
melted butter for serving
lemon wedges for serving
baguette cut into 2- to 3-inch slices

**1.** Fill a large stockpot half-full with water. Add beer, crab boil seasoning and salt. Bring to a boil over high heat.

**2.** Add potatoes and cook partially covered for about 15 to18 minutes, until the potatoes are tender. Using a strainer or basket, remove the potatoes to a large oven-safe bowl and place this in a warm oven.

**3.** Bring the liquid back to a boil. Add the crab and crayfish, cooking until they are bright red, about 7 minutes. Add the corn, shrimp and sausage, and cook for another 7 to 10 minutes. Carefully drain the cooked ingredients.

***To serve:***
Cover a table with newspaper. Put melted butter into individual bowls and pass around the Old Bay® seasoning for sprinkling. Pour everything in the middle of the table and dig in!

*Note: **If your stockpot is not large enough to hold everything, you can cook in batches, or cook in two large pots, dividing the ingredients. Keep the cooked food warm in an oven at 225º.***

*Serves 6 generously*

## BUYING FRESH CLAMS AND MUSSELS

When buying clams and mussels be sure that they have
tightly closed shells. If a shell is slightly open, it should
close when gently tapped. If it doesn't shut, this means
that the clam is dead and should not be purchased. Avoid
clams or mussels with broken, chipped or damaged shells.
I find that the smaller the clam, the better the flavor—this
does not necessarily hold true for mussels, however. Never
store live clams or mussels in a closed plastic bag, because
they'll suffocate. Instead, place them in a bowl and cover
them with a damp cloth. You can keep them alive this way
in the refrigerator for several days (I've kept them alive in
the refrigerator for as long as a week). When you are ready
to use them, scrub the clams or mussels with a stiff brush
under cold running water. Most mussels sold today are
farmed and come fully cleaned. If your mussels are wild,
however, you'll need to de-beard them: Simply use your
fingers to pull out the clump of hair-like strands. After
cooking clams or mussels, discard any that do not open.

# san francisco cioppino

*If San Francisco has a signature dish, this is it.*
*Be sure to serve lots of good bread to sop up the delicious broth.*

2 Dungeness crab, cleaned and cracked (cooked or uncooked)
1 pound large shrimp in shell, leaving tail intact
12 to18 small mussels or clams in shell (or a combination of both)
$^1/_2$ pound scallops
1 cup onion, chopped
1 green pepper, chopped
$^3/_4$ cup olive oil
1 tablespoon minced garlic
3 $^1/_2$ cups canned Italian plum tomatoes (fresh may be substituted)
1 $^3/_4$ cups tomato puree
1 $^1/_2$ to 2 cups white wine, or red wine if you prefer
1$^1/_2$ teaspoons red pepper flakes
$^1/_2$ teaspoon dried basil
1 $^1/_2$ teaspoons salt
2 teaspoons freshly ground black pepper
minced flat-leaf parsley (garnish)

**1.** Sauté the onion and green pepper in olive oil, in a large soup pot, over medium heat until the onions and green pepper are softened. Add the garlic and cook for 1 more minute. Stir in the tomatoes, tomato puree, wine, red pepper flakes, basil, salt and pepper. Bring to a boil, and simmer for 1 hour. This can be made up to 1 day ahead of serving.

**2.** When ready to serve, add the crab, shrimp, clams, mussels and scallops. Bring to a boil, reduce heat to low, and simmer 10 to 12 minutes, covered.

**3.** Discard any clams or mussels that did not open during the cooking process. Serve in large heated bowls, and garnish with parsley.

*Note:* **Serve with a bowl for the shells.**

*Serves 4*

# paupiette de saumon au crabe

*I had given up on a good crab stuffing recipe for fish. I tried a great many, and never found or developed one that I thought was worthy of including in a cookbook. Well, that is until I had the Paupiette de Saumon au Crab at C'est Si Bon in Port Angeles, Washington. Upon tasting this dish, I knew it was the recipe I'd been searching for. But would they share their recipe with me? Owners Michele and Norbert Juhasz most generously did. This outstanding dish is one of my all-time favorite crab recipes. This can be assembled ahead of time and then baked just before serving.*

3 tablespoons butter
$1/3$ cup thinly sliced leeks (I've also used scallions with great results)
6 ounces crabmeat ($3/4$ Cup)
1 pound boned salmon fillet, with skin removed 7 to 8 inches wide*
2 cups dry vermouth
$1/2$ cup whipping cream
salt
freshly ground black pepper
2 tablespoons minced fresh chives (garnish)
lemon wedges (optional)

**1.** Preheat oven to 450°.

**2.** Melt 1 tablespoon of butter in a large oven-proof skillet, over medium-low heat. Add the leeks and cook them until softened, about 5 minutes. Transfer the leeks to a bowl. Add the remaining 2 tablespoons of butter to the pan. Melt the butter, add the crabmeat, and stir and cook until warm, about 2 minutes. Push the crabmeat to one side of pan and set aside.

**3.** Rinse and pat dry the salmon. Holding a knife at a 45° angle, cut the salmon flesh crosswise, off the skin, into $1/4$-inch slices. You should have about 12 slices.

**4.** Lay out the salmon slices, and spoon about 1 tablespoon of crab mixture onto the wide end of each. Starting at that end, roll the salmon tightly around crab. Place the salmon rolls, seam-side down, in the skillet.

**5.** Pour the vermouth around the salmon rolls, and bake the fish until it is opaque but still moist-looking in the center (about 12-15 minutes). With a slotted spoon, transfer salmon rolls to plates, cover loosely with foil and let stand in a warm place.

**6.** Add cream and reserved leek to pan and boil over high heat until liquid is slightly thickened and reduced to about 1 $^1/_3$ cups, 8 to 9 minutes. Season to taste with salt and pepper. Spoon sauce equally around salmon rolls and garnish with chives and lemon wedges if desired.

*Serves 4*

*Note: When slicing the salmon and assembling this recipe, it can be less than eye-pleasing, but don't fear! This bakes into a beautiful dish. What you put in the oven looks nothing like the end result. My good friend Linda Kaminski often makes this dish. Instead of the slicing and rolling, she simply makes diagonal slits in the salmon and stuffs the crab into the slits, with wonderful results.*

"And now with some pleasure I find that it's seven; and must cook dinner."

*-Virginia Woolf*

# mendo bistro's award-winning crab cakes

*Chef / Owner Nicholas Petti of Mendo Bistro in Fort Bragg was deemed unbeatable in the Mendocino Crab Festival's annual crab-cake cook-off with these crab cakes, so they finally made him a judge. At the Bistro, they like to serve these fabulous crab cakes with a simple cabbage salad, which allows the crisp, green cabbage flavor to marry with the vinegar, serving as a perfect foil for the rich crab meat and creamy tarragon aioli.*

**For the Tarragon aioli:**
2 egg yolks
3 cloves garlic
juice of 1 lemon
$1/2$ teaspoon salt
dash Tabasco® sauce
$1/4$ cup very hot water
2 cups olive oil
$1/2$ bunch tarragon, finely chopped

**For the Cabbage Salad:**
1 head green cabbage
sea salt
1 bunch chives, finely chopped
$1/3$ cup champagne vinegar

**For the Crab Cakes:**
1 $1/2$ pounds Dungeness crabmeat
$3/4$ cup panko bread crumbs, plus additional for outer coating
2 scallions, finely chopped
Oil for sautéing

*Prepare the aioli:*
Blend the egg yolks, garlic, lemon, salt and Tabasco® sauce in a food processor or blender. Pour in hot water and process for 15 seconds. With the machine still running, slowly drizzle in the oil until a mayonnaise consistency is reached. Stir in the tarragon. Set aside.

***Prepare the salad:***
**1.** Remove the outer leaves and core from cabbage, and slice thinly. Toss with a liberal amount of salt and let the cabbage sit for 30 minutes.

**2.** Drain off any liquid from the cabbage, and combine with chives and vinegar.

***Prepare the Crab Cakes:***
**1.** Combine the crabmeat, bread crumbs and scallions. Add $^1/_2$ cup aioli and test the mixture to see how well it holds together. If necessary, add up to an additional $^1/_4$ cup of aioli. Do not overwork ingredients. Cakes should be loose and just barely hold together. Form the mixture into cakes about 3 inches in diameter, and place one side in additional bread crumbs.

**2.** Heat the oil in a medium sauté pan over medium-high heat, until just smoking. Place the cakes, bread-crumb side down, in the pan. Sauté them until they're golden, and then carefully turn them over. Lower the heat to medium, and sauté until the cakes are heated through.

***To Serve:***
Serve the crab cakes on the cabbage salad and drizzle with additional aioli.

*Serves 4-6*

# macadamia-crusted
# crab cakes with mango salsa

*These crab cakes transport me to tropical places. The mango salsa is the creation of my son, Josh.*

**For the Mango Salsa:**
2 fresh mangos, cut into $^1/_4$-inch cubes
1 cup diced red onion
1 jalapeno pepper, stemmed, seeded and minced
$^1/_2$ teaspoon chili powder
$^1/_2$ teaspoon garlic powder
$^1/_4$ cup fresh lime juice
2 tablespoons honey or 1 teaspoon sugar
$^1/_4$ cup cilantro
$^1/_2$ teaspoon salt
$^1/_2$ teaspoon freshly ground black pepper

**For the Crab Cakes:**
$^1/_4$ cup mayonnaise
1 egg, beaten
$^1/_2$ teaspoon dry mustard
2 tablespoons minced cilantro
$^1/_2$ teaspoon salt
3 to 5 drops hot pepper sauce
$^1/_4$ cup minced red pepper
$^1/_4$ cup minced scallions (white and green parts)
2 tablespoons fresh lime juice
1 pound crabmeat, excess moisture squeezed out
$^1/_2$ cup finely crushed saltines
$^1/_2$ cup dry bread crumbs (Japanese panko may also be used)
$^1/_2$ cup macadamia nuts, crushed
3 tablespoons butter
3 tablespoons oil

*Prepare the salsa:*
Combine the mango, onion, pepper, chili powder, garlic powder, lime juice, honey (or sugar), cilantro, salt and pepper in a small bowl, and mix gently. Refrigerate to allow the flavors to blend. Serve at room temperature.

*Prepare the crab cakes:*
**1.** Whisk mayonnaise, egg, mustard, cilantro, salt, pepper sauce, red pepper, scallions and lime juice, in a large bowl. Gently fold in crab and saltines with a spatula and mix gently to combine.

**2.** Shape the crab mixture into 6 cakes about 3 inches wide. Refrigerate them for at least 1 hour before proceeding.

**3.** Mix together the bread crumbs and macadamia nuts on a plate. Coat the crab cakes with this mixture.

**4.** Heat the butter and oil in a large skillet, over medium-low heat. Add the crab cakes and cook about 5 to 7 minutes on each side, turning only once, until golden brown.
Serve with mango salsa.

*Serves 4*

## Mangos

Mangos are the world's most consumed fruit and were originally cultivated in India over 6,000 years ago. When buying Mangos look for smooth unblemished skin. Avoid those with bruised or dry and shriveled skin. The ripeness of mangos can be determined by either smelling or squeezing. A ripe mango will have a full, fruity aroma and will yield to gentle pressure but should not be overly mushy. Mangos continue to ripen after picking. Store at room temperature for 2-5 days to ripen. While a mango will not ripen in the refrigerator, it can be kept chilled there once ripe. Store cut mangos in a plastic bag for no more than 3 days.

# sautéed soft-shell crab with wine, lemon & caper pan sauce

*This tasty dish is basically my adaptation of crab meuniere. The smaller the crab, the better. This is prepared with clarified butter, which can be made ahead of time.*

4 soft-shell crab
$1/2$ cup flour, for dredging
8 tablespoons clarified butter*
4 tablespoons lemon juice
4 tablespoons white wine
$1/2$ teaspoon salt
$1/4$ teaspoon freshly ground black pepper
1 tablespoon tiny capers
1 scallion, minced
lemon wedges for serving

**Prepare the Crab:**
**1.** Pat the crab dry with paper towels (this helps prevent splattering). Dredge crab in flour, shaking off excess.

**2.** Heat the clarified butter in a large heavy skillet over medium-high heat until hot, but not smoking. Add the crab, skin-side down, and cook until it turns reddish brown, about 3 minutes. Turn the crab over, and cook 2 to 3 minutes more. Transfer the crab to a warmed serving dish.

**Prepare the Sauce:**
**1.** Add lemon juice, wine, salt, pepper and capers to the pan. As soon as the mixture bubbles, cook for 2 minutes.

**2.** Spoon the sauce over the crab. Sprinkle minced scallion over the top, and serve with lemon wedges.

***\* Clarified butter has a higher smoke point, allowing you to cook at higher temperatures without burning. Clarifying removes the milk solids and water.***

## Clarified Butter

Melt 1 ¹/₂ sticks unsalted butter slowly in a pan. Simmer over low heat, without stirring, until the milk solids have separated and sink to the bottom. Other impurities will rise to the surface, while the butterfat in the middle layer becomes very clear.

Remove the pan from the heat and skim off the foam with a spoon. Then carefully ladle the clarified butterfat into a separate container. Be careful to leave the solids behind.

# soft shell crab in tempura batter with ponzu dipping sauce

*This Japanese specialty is a natural for soft-shell crab. The secret to its light crispy batter and delicate crunch is ice water, lumpy batter and making the batter at the last possible moment. The ponzu sauce is the perfect dipping sauce, with its zesty citrus flavors. Ponzu sauce may also be purchased.*

**Ponzu sauce:**
$1/4$ cup lime juice
$1/4$ cup lemon juice
$1/2$ cup soy sauce
$1/4$ cup rice vinegar
1 $1/2$ tablespoons sugar
$1/4$ cup scallion thinly sliced (mostly green part)

**Crab:**
4 large soft-shell crab
flour for dusting
canola or olive oil for frying

**Tempura Batter:**
1 egg
1 cup flour
1 cup ice water

*Prepare Ponzu Sauce:*
In a medium bowl, whisk the lime juice, lemon juice, soy sauce, vinegar, sugar and scallions, until well blended.

Preheat the oven to 225°.

*Prepare Crab:*
1. Blot the crab with paper towels to remove any excess moisture. Lightly dust the crab with flour, shaking off any excess.

**2.** Begin heating the oil (to 350°) in a deep fryer or a large heavy sauce pan, with enough oil to completely submerge the crab, cooking two at a time.

***Tempura Batter:***
**1.** In a small bowl, whisk the egg with a fork and pour in the ice water, mixing gently. Add the flour all at once, stroke a few times with a fork, until the ingredients are loosely combined. The batter should be lumpy.

**2.** Dip the crab in the batter and coat well. Carefully place the crab in the hot oil and cook them until golden, about 2 to 4 minutes. Remove the crab and place them on a plate covered with paper towels. Place in a warmed oven, while preparing the remaining crab.

*Note:* **If you don't have a thermometer to test the oil, try this: Place a drop of batter into the oil and see if the batter quickly floats to the surface. If it does, the oil is hot enough. If it takes its time, let the oil heat longer.**

*Serves 2*

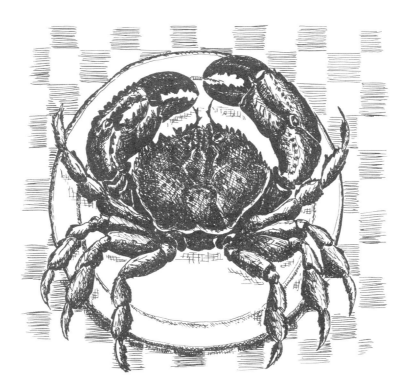

# spanish crab & artichoke paella

*This festive dish makes for a gorgeously dramatic presentation. Paella is Spain's signature dish. The name paella comes from the pan the dish is cooked in. The pan is circular and shallow, with a handle on each side. You don't need a paella pan—a wide shallow skillet will work just fine. Rioja wine or sangria go wonderfully with this dish.*

$^1/_4$ cup water
$^1/_3$ cup olive oil
1 cup chopped onions
2 tablespoons chopped garlic
1 cup chopped red bell pepper
2 medium tomatoes, chopped
2 cups long grain rice*
1 teaspoon salt
$^1/_2$ teaspoon freshly ground black pepper
2 teaspoons Spanish paprika
2 cups chicken broth
1 cup white wine
$^1/_2$ teaspoon saffron threads, crumbled
$^1/_2$ cup frozen sweet peas, thawed
10 stone-crab claws or 1 $^1/_2$ pounds crab legs
12 medium shrimp, cleaned and peeled, tails intact
12 small mussels, scrubbed and de-bearded
12 small clams, scrubbed
$^1/_2$ pound linguisa (firm chorizo) or other sausage, sliced and cooked
1 (9-ounce) package frozen artichoke hearts, thawed
lemon wedges for serving

**1.** Preheat the oven to 375°.

**2.** Heat $^1/_4$ cup water, not to the boiling but just hot, in a cup in the microwave. Add saffron and set aside.

*Prepare the Sofrito:*
**1.** Heat the oil over medium heat in a large, oven-proof, 12- to 14-inch skillet. Add the onion, garlic and red bell pepper, sautéing until softened (about 5 to 7 minutes).

**2.** Add the tomato and rice, stirring constantly until the rice is transulant. Add the salt, pepper, Spanish paprika, chicken broth, wine and saffron broth mixture. Reduce the heat to low and simmer, stirring occasionally, for about 10 to 15 minutes, until the rice is no longer soupy, but a sufficient amount of liquid remains to continue cooking the dish in the oven.

*To Assemble:*
**1.** Stir in the peas. Arrange the crab, shrimp, mussels, clams, sausage and artichokes on top of the rice mixture. Loosely tent with foil.

**2.** Place the skillet in the oven, and cook for about 15 minutes. Then remove it from the oven, take of the foil tent, and discard any clams or mussels that did not open. Place the foil tent back on, and let the dish cool for 5 minutes.

*To Serve:*
Serve the paella in its pan, at the center of the table.

**\*Using long grain rice for paella goes completely against the tradition in Spain, where short grain rice, such as arborio or pearl, is used. I just happen to prefer long grain rice for paella. Use what you prefer.**

*Serves 4-6*

*Saffron is the yellow-orange stigma(the stamen of the female flower) from the purple crocus (crocus sativus). Each crocus has only three stigma, and must be carefully hand-picked, making this an expensive ingredient. Luckily it only takes a few threads. If you don't see saffron in the spice section, ask the manager it's often kept behind lock and key*

"A man who is stingy with saffron is capable of seducing his own grandmother."
*-Norman Douglas, English Writer (1868-1952)*

perfect
accompaniments
& the perfect
ending

# PERFECT ACCOMPANIMENTS
## & THE PERFECT ENDING

*grandma's coleslaw*

*grilled corn on the cob*

*old fashioned potato salad*

*tossed green salad with herbed croutons*

*parsley red potatoes*

*key lime pie*

# grandma's coleslaw

*My husband says his grandmother's coleslaw is the best coleslaw ever made. Fortunately, his sister Jennifer (who also illustrated this book) had the recipe and continues to make this delicious coleslaw.*

4 cups chopped green cabbage (chop the cabbage by hand; do not use a food processor.)
$^1/_2$ medium green pepper, diced
3 scallions, diced

I like to use at least one of the following for color and added flavor:

$^1/_2$ carrot, grated
1 cup quartered cherry tomatoes
$^1/_2$ cup seeded and diced cucumber
1 cup chopped red cabbage

**Dressing:**
$^1/_2$ cup mayonnaise
$^1/_2$ milk or half-and-half
$^1/_4$ cup apple cider vinegar
1 tablespoon sugar
salt
freshly ground black pepper

**1.** Combine the carrot, tomatoes, cucumber and cabbage in a medium bowl, and set aside.

Mix mayonnaise and milk (or half-and-half) in a small bowl, until smooth and lump free. Stir in vinegar and sugar. At this point, taste and correct—the dressing should be very tangy, sweet and sour. Add salt and pepper, seasoning to taste.

**3.** Pour the dressing onto the vegetables and toss. The salad improves in flavor if made several hours ahead or the night before. Toss again just before serving.

*Serves 4*

# grilled corn on the cob

*The slightly smoky and charred flavor of grilled corn-on-the-cob is irresistible.*

1 to 2 ears of sweet corn per person
salt
freshly ground black pepper
butter melted

**1.** Soak the corn in cold water for 20 minutes. Remove all but the last layer of the husk, leaving one layer. With scissors, snip the silk off the end of the corn.

**2.** Grill the corn, turning about every 2 minutes, until done, about 8 to 10 minutes. Once done, remove the remaining husk and silk.

**3.** Season the corn to taste, with salt, pepper and butter. Serve immediately.

# old-fashioned potato salad

*This is it! Potato salad just like you remember.*
*This is a great make-ahead dish, as it only gets better after being refrigerated.*

16 eggs, hard boiled
5 pounds russet potatoes, peeled and cut into 1-inch cubes (11 cups cooked and cubed)
$1/2$ cup white wine vinegar
$1/2$ cup extra virgin olive oil
1 teaspoon salt
$1/2$ teaspoon freshly ground black pepper
$1^1/2$ cups mayonnaise, homemade or store-bought
$1/2$ cup sour cream
$1/4$ cup Dijon mustard
$1/8$ cup yellow mustard
$1/4$ teaspoon ground cayenne pepper
$1/2$ teaspoon sugar
1 tablespoon Old Bay® Seasoning
1 cup chopped celery
1 cup scallions, chopped (both green and white parts) (red onion may be substituted)

Paprika (for presentation)

**1.** Chop 15 of the hard-boiled eggs. Slice the remaining one, and set it aside for garnishing.

**2.** Place the potatoes in a large saucepan, and cover with cold water. Bring to a boil, reduce the heat, and simmer until tender, about 10 minutes (careful not to overcook).

**3.** While the potatoes are cooking, whisk together the vinegar, olive oil, salt and pepper in a small bowl or large measuring cup. Drain potatoes in a colander, transfer them to a large bowl, and toss them with the vinegar mixture.

**4.** Whisk together the mayonnaise, sour cream, mustards, cayenne pepper, sugar, and Old Bay® Seasoning in a small bowl. Taste and adjust seasoning as needed.

**5.** Add the celery, scallions and chopped eggs to the potatoes. Toss to combine. Add the mayonnaise mixture to potatoes and stir gently to combine. Refrigerate.

**6.** When ready to serve, place the egg slices on top of the potato salad, and sprinkle the paprika over the top.

*Serves 8-10*

### Perfect Hard-boiled Boiled eggs

Place room- temperature eggs in a pot of cold water. (If you put them in hot water, It's the quick change in temperature may that causes the heat source. After sitting for 15 minutes, the eggs are done. Gently crack the shell and peel under cold running water.

# tossed green salad with herbed croutons

*The herbed croutons make this simple salad extraordinary.*

**Herbed Croutons:**
$^1/_4$ cup olive oil
2 ($^3/_4$-inch-thick) country bread slices, crusts cut off, bread cut into $^3/_4$-inch cubes
(about 3 cups total)
2 garlic cloves, minced
1 teaspoon dried oregano, crumbled
1 teaspoon dried basil, crumbled
1 teaspoon dried thyme, crumbled
salt
freshly ground black pepper
1/4 cup finely grated Parmigiano-Reagiano cheese

**Vinaigrette:**
$^1/_4$ cup champagne vinegar or white wine vinegar
3 cloves garlic, mashed or 2 shallots, mashed
1 tablespoon Dijon mustard
$^1/_2$ teaspoon salt
$^1/_4$ teaspoon freshly ground black pepper
1 teaspoon sugar
$^3/_4$ cup canola oil or light olive oil

**Salad:**
2 heads romaine lettuce
2 heads red leaf lettuce
1 cup halved cherry tomatoes
1 red onion, sliced into thin rings

*Prepare the croutons:*
**1.** Heat oil over medium heat in a 12-inch skillet, add bread cubes, and cook bread, stirring occasionally until golden on all sides, about 5-7 minutes. Add garlic, oregano, basil, thyme, salt and pepper. Reduce heat to low and cook, stirring another 2 minutes.

**2.** Remove skillet from heat and add Parmigiano-Reggiano, tossing croutons to coat well. Croutons may be made 3 days ahead and kept in a sealable plastic bag in a cool dry place. Croutons also freeze well.

***Prepare the vinaigrette:***
Whisk the vinegar, oil, garlic, mustard, salt, pepper and sugar together in a small bowl. Slowly drizzle in the oil, whisking constantly until it is fully incorporated. Taste and adjust the seasonings. This can be stored up to a week in the in refrigerator.

***Prepare the salad:***
**1.** Chop, wash and dry the lettuces. In a large salad bowl, combine the lettuces, tomatoes and onion.

**2.** When ready to serve the salad, toss greens with dressing, and season with salt and pepper (do this right before serving or salad will become soggy). Top with croutons.

*Serves 4-6*

# parsley red potatoes

1$^1$/$_2$ cups water
1 pound small red potatoes
1 tablespoon butter
1 tablespoon chopped flat-leaf parsley
salt
freshly ground black pepper

**1.** Bring the water to a boil in the bottom of a steamer. Place the potatoes in one layer in the top of the steamer, cover and reduce heat to medium. Cook for about 25 to 30 minutes until tender.

**2.** Remove the potatoes, and toss with butter and parsley. Season to taste with salt and pepper.

*Serves 4*

"An unwatched pot boils immediately."
*-H.F. Ellis*

# *key lime pie*

*The perfect ending. What could be better than a refreshing slice of Key lime pie?*
*If you can't find Key limes, you'll also get great results from regular limes.*
*If possible, refrain from using bottled lime juice—the results may disappoint you.*

### Crust
1$^1$/$_4$ cups graham cracker crumbs (11 graham crackers processed or blended to fine crumbs)
$^1$/$_3$ cup sugar
5 tablespoons melted butter

### Filling
4 large egg yolks
4 teaspoons grated lime zest
1(14 ounce) can sweetened condensed milk
$^1$/$_2$ cup fresh-squeezed lime juice (3-5 limes, depending on size)

### Topping
1 cup heavy or whipping cream
$^1$/$_4$ cup sugar
1 teaspoon vanilla
1 lime, thinly sliced for garnish (optional)

***Prepare the crust:***
**1.** Pre-heat oven to 325°.

**2.** Mix graham cracker crumbs, sugar and butter in a medium bowl with a fork, until well blended. Press mixture into the bottom and up the sides of a 9-inch pie pan, to form an even crust.

**3.** Bake on center rack about 12 minutes or until crust is lightly browned. Leave the oven on.

***Prepare the filling:***
**1.** Beat egg yolks and lime zest with electric mixer at high speed, until very fluffy (about 5 minutes). Gradually add the condensed milk and continue to beat until thick. Lower speed and add lime juice.

**2.** Pour mixture into cooled crust. Bake for about 15 minutes or until the center is set, but still wiggles. Be careful not to over-bake the pie or it will be "rubbery". Remove from oven and cool to room temperature. Refrigerate for at least 3 hours.

***Prepare the topping:***
**1.** Whip cream in a medium bowl with an electric mixer. Once soft peaks appear, slowly add sugar, whipping until almost stiff. Add vanilla and stir.

**2.** Spread gently over Key lime pie, and garnish with lime slices, if desired.

# sauces, salsas & flavored butters

# SAUCES, SALSAS & FLAVORED BUTTERS

homemade mayonnaise

avocado mayonnaise

bloody mary cocktail sauce

salsa fresca

roasted corn salsa

mango salsa

creamy chipotle sauce

kelly's special sauce

tarragon aioli

tartar sauce

louis dressing

roasted red pepper sauce

roasted red bell pepper sauce

red pepper cream sauce

lemon aioli

mustard sauce

spicy cocktail cauce

sesame-ginger sauce

key lime hollandaise sauce

creamy lemon vinagrette

classic white sauce

orange basil butter

chili japapeño butter

citrus butter

drawn butter

garlic black pepper butter

lemon anchovy tutter

lemon chervil butter

lemon chive butter

lemon pepper butter

lime cilantro butter

spicy herbed butter

tarragon butter

# homemade mayonnaise

*This mayonnaise will keep for up to a week in the refrigerator.*

2 egg yolks
1 whole egg
1 tablespoon Dijon mustard
$^3/_4$ teaspoon salt
freshly ground black pepper to taste
$^1/_8$ teaspoon sugar
pinch cayenne pepper
3 tablespoons fresh squeezed lemon juice
2 cups vegetable oil (I like to use 1 cup of canola and 1 cup of olive oil)

Combine the egg yolks, whole egg, mustard salt, black pepper, sugar, cayenne pepper, and lemon juice in a blender or food processor. Blend or process for 15 seconds. Now, with the motor still running, slowly drizzle in 1/4 cup of oil (use moderately high blender speed). As the mixture begins to thicken, continue adding the oil in a fine steady stream. Stop the motor and scrape the mixture down from sides of blender cup or work bowl as needed.

*Makes about 2$^1/_2$ cups*

# avocado mayonnaise

1 large avocados pitted, quartered
4 tablespoons mayonnaise
1 tablespoon fresh lime juice
$^1/_2$ teaspoon hot pepper sauce
salt
freshly ground black pepper

Puree the avocado, mayonnaise, lime juice and hot pepper sauce in a blender. Season to taste with salt and pepper. This should be served within 4 hours, or it may become discolored. Give it a good stir prior to serving.

*Makes about 3/4 cup*

# bloody mary cocktail sauce

$^1/_2$ cup tomato juice
1 teaspoon horseradish
$^1/_4$ cup chili sauce
$^1/_2$ teaspoon black pepper
dash of sugar
1 tablespoons fresh lemon juice
1 teaspoon Worcestershire sauce
1 tablespoon olive oil
2 teaspoons citron-flavored vodka or lemon-flavored vodka

In a blender or food processor, puree the tomato juice, horseradish, chili sauce, pepper, sugar, lemon juice, Worcestershire sauce, olive oil and vodka. Refrigerate until ready to use.

*Makes about 1 cup*

# salsa fresca

2 cups tomatoes, diced
$^1/_2$ cup white onion, finely chopped
3 scallions, finely chopped
2 fresh jalapeno chiles*, stemmed, seeded and minced (I like to use 1 red and 1 green)
$^1/_3$ cup minced cilantro
2 to 3 tablespoons fresh lime juice
1 teaspoon salt
freshly ground black pepper to taste
$^1/_8$ teaspoon sugar

Prepare Salsa Fresca by combining all ingredients in a bowl. Mix thoroughly.

**\* Use less jalapeno pepper if you like it less spicy.**

*Makes about 3 cups*

*In the early 1990's, salsa surpassed ketchup in sales, claiming the title as the world's most popular condiment. For the best salsa, chop everything by hand. Salsa is best eaten on the day it is made, and should be eaten within 2 to 3 days, at most. To refresh a salsa, put the salsa in a pan, cover it with water (about 1/4 cup) and simmer it for 10 minutes. Let it -cool and put it through the blender. Viola! You've got a brand new salsa.*

# roasted corn salsa

1 cup of roasted corn kernels (1 to 2 ears)
2 tablespoons olive oil
$^1/_4$ cup chopped scallions
$^1/_4$ cup chopped red bell pepper
3 tablespoons chopped fresh cilantro
2 tablespoons fresh lime juice
2 plum tomatoes, finely chopped
2 jalapeno peppers, stemmed, seeded and minced
$^1/_2$ teaspoon salt
$^1/_4$ teaspoon black pepper

Husk corn, baste with olive oil. Grill or broil 4 inches from heat till golden, about 10 minutes. Put kernels in bowl, stir in all ingredients. Taste and adjust seasoning if needed. Refrigerate at least one hour prior to serving. Serve cold or at room temperature.

*Makes about 3 cups.*

# mango salsa

2 fresh mangos cut into $^1/_4$ inch cubes
1 cup red onion diced
1 jalapeno steamed, seeded and minced
$^1/_2$ teaspoon good quality chili powder
$^1/_2$ teaspoon garlic powder
$^1/_4$ cup fresh lime juice
2 tablespoons honey or 1 teaspoon sugar
$^1/_4$ cup cilantro
$^1/_2$ teaspoon salt
$^1/_2$ teaspoon black pepper

In a small bowl combine all the ingredients, mix gently. Refrigerate to allow flavors to blend. Serve at room temperature.

*Makes about 3 cups.*

# creamy chipotle sauce

$1/2$ cup mayonnaise
$1/2$ cup sour cream
1 tablespoon minced chipotle chiles in adobe sauce
2 teaspoons fresh lime juice
$1/2$ teaspoon garlic powder
1 tablespoon cilantro minced
$1/2$ teaspoon salt

Combine all ingredients in a small bowl and stir until well-blended.
Refrigerate until ready to use.

*Makes about 1 cup*


# kelly's special sauce

1 cup mayonnaise (Best Foods)
$1/2$ cup ketchup
$1 \ 1/2$ teaspoons Worcestershire sauce
$1/8$ teaspoon cayenne
$1/8$ teaspoon granulated garlic
$1/4$ teaspoon black pepper
$1/8$ teaspoon McCormick's Salad Supreme Seasoning
$1/8$ cup red wine vinegar

In a small bowl, whisk mayonnaise until smooth to eliminate lumps. Add ketchup stir well and
add remaining ingredients mixing well. Refrigerate until ready to use.

*Makes about 2 cupss*

# tarragon aioli

2 egg yolks
3 cloves garlic
Juice of 1 lemon
$^1/_2$ teaspoon salt
 Dash Tabasco sauce
$^1/_4$ cup very hot water
2 cups olive oil
$^1/_4$  bunch tarragon, finely chopped.

In a food processor or blender, places all ingredients up to and including Tabasco and run the machine. Pour in hot water and process for 15 seconds. With machine running, slowly drizzle in oil until a mayonnaise consistency is reached. Stir in tarragon. Refrigerate until ready to serve.

*Makes about 2 $^1/_2$  cup.*

# tartar sauce

$^1/_4$ cup chopped red onion
$^1/_4$ cup roughly chopped capers
$^1/_4$ cup chopped cornichons, plus 2 tablespoons of the juice
3 cups  mayonnaise
$^1/_2$ teaspoon kosher salt
$^1/_2$ teaspoon freshly ground black pepper

Blend the mayonnaise, Worcestershire sauce, mustard, capers, lemon juice, relish, shallots (or onions) and hot sauce. Refrigerate the sauce for at least 1 hour. This will keep in the refrigerator for up to 1 week.

# louis dressing

1 cup mayonnaise (homemade or store bought)
$^1/_4$ cup chili sauce
3 tablespoons minced scallion (green onion)
1 tablespoon lemon juice
1 teaspoon Worcestershire sauce
Pinch cayenne
$^1/_4$ teaspoon salt
$^1/_2$ teaspoon pepper

Whisk together the mayonnaise, chili sauce, scallions, lemon juice, Worcestershire sauce, cayenne pepper, salt and pepper in a large bowl. Refrigerate the dressing for at least 1 hour

*Makes about 1 $^1/_2$ cups.*

# roasted red pepper sauce

1 cup mayonnaise
1-8 ounce jar fire roasted red peppers
1 tablespoon fresh lemon juice
$^1/_4$ teaspoon cayenne
$^1/_4$ cup sliced almonds
1 teaspoon garlic powder

Combine all ingredients in a blender or food processor and blend until smooth. Refrigerate until ready to serve.

*Makes about 2 cups.*

# roasted red bell pepper sauce

*This is the sauce served with crab stuffed roasted poblanos.*
*This sauce is also delicious over grilled chicken and fish.*

2-3 large red bell peppers
1 tablespoon olive oil
$1/4$  cup chopped shallots
2 garlic cloves, minced
1 jalapeno pepper, seeded, minced
$1/2$ teaspoon cayenne
$1/8$ teaspoon sugar
1 cup low-salt chicken broth

**1.** Char bell peppers over gas flame or in broiler until blackened on all sides. Enclose in paper bag 10 minutes. Peel, seed, and coarsely chop bell peppers.

**2.** Heat oil in medium skillet over medium heat. Add shallots, garlic, and chili; sauté until shallots are soft, about 5 minutes.

**3.** Transfer mixture to blender; add bell peppers and chicken broth, cayenne and sugar . Puree until smooth. Season to taste with salt and pepper. (Can be made 1 day ahead. Re-heat before serving.)

*Makes about 2 $1/3$  cups.*

# red pepper cream sauce

2 tablespoons butter
1 shallot, finely chopped
2 cloves garlic, finely chopped
4 roasted red peppers*
1 cup white wine
1 cup chicken broth
1 cup heavy cream

**1.** Sauté the shallots in butter for about 3 minutes. Add garlic and roasted peppers, sautéing for about 3 more minutes. Add wine and cook until reduced by half. Add broth and reduce by half, and then add cream, once again reducing by half (be careful not to boil the sauce).

**2.** Transfer the sauce to a blender and puree until smooth.

**3.** Return the pureed sauce to low heat and whisk in the butter. Season to taste with salt and pepper.

*Makes about 3 $1/4$ cups.*

# lemon aioli

2 egg yolks at room temperature
$1/4$ cup fresh squeezed lemon juice
1 tablespoon grated lemon zest
2 small cloves garlic minced**
$1/2$ teaspoon salt
$1/8$ teaspoon white pepper
$1/8$ teaspoon cayenne pepper
1 teaspoon Dijon mustard
$1/2$ teaspoon sugar
2 cups oil (I like to use 1 cup of olive and 1 cup canola)

In a blender or food processor, combine egg yolks, lemon juice, zest, garlic, salt, white pepper, cayenne, mustard, & sugar. Blend or process about 10 seconds, With blender running slowly add oil in a slow stream blending until an emulsion forms. Stop blending or processing once all the oil has been added. Taste and adjust seasoning if needed. Refrigerate until ready to use.

*\* For a quicker version of the lemon aioli. Combine 2 cups of mayonnaise with lemon juice, lemon zest, cayenne and Dijon mustard. Typically aioli contains more garlic than I included in this recipe. I wanted to let all the lemon flavors shine through. If you're so inclined add 3-5 additional cloves of garlic.*

# mustard sauce

$1/2$ cup sour cream
$1/2$ cup mayonnaise
$1/2$ cup spicy brown mustard
1 tablespoon honey
$3/4$ tablespoon Worcestershire sauce
1 teaspoon dry mustard

Combine the sour cream, mayonnaise, brown mustard, honey, Worcestershire sauce and dry mustard in a small bowl, and stir until well-blended. Refrigerate until ready to use.

# spicy cocktail sauce

2 cups ketchup
1 $^1/_2$ tablespoons prepared horseradish
2 tablespoons Worcestershire sauce
1 tablespoon fresh lemon juice
1 teaspoon black pepper

Combine all ingredients in a small bowl, stirring well. Refrigerate until ready to use.

*Makes about 2 cups.*

# sesame-ginger sauce

$^1/_3$ cup soy sauce
1 teaspoon Chinese hot mustard or more if you like it hotter
2 tablespoons each lemon and lime juice (this is optional)
1 tablespoon sugar
1 teaspoon Asian sesame oil
1 teaspoon ginger

In a small bowl, add the soy sauce then whisk in remaining ingredients.

*Makes about $^1/_2$ cup.*

# key lime hollandaise sauce

1 cup butter
3 egg yolks
$^1/_2$ teaspoon salt
Dash of cayenne pepper
2 tablespoons key lime juice (regular limes may be used or lemons if you prefer)

Melt the butter over medium heat until bubbling, being careful not to brown. Place egg yolks, salt and pepper in a blender or food processor. Blend at high speed for a few seconds, until you have a smooth frothy mixture. Still at a high speed, start adding the hot butter in a thin steady stream. The sauce will start thickening as you add the butter. When half the butter has been added, add the lime juice (or lemon juice). Continue until all the butter has been used.

*Makes about 2 cups.*

# creamy lemon vinaigrette

1 shallot, minced
$^1/_2$ cup fresh lemon juice
1 tablespoon grated lemon peel
1 tablespoon champagne vinegar
$^1/_2$ teaspoon Dijon mustard
$^1/_2$ teaspoon sugar
$^3/_4$ teaspoon salt
$^1/_4$ teaspoon freshly ground black pepper
$^1/_4$ cup canola oil
$^1/_4$ cup extra virgin olive oil

Combine the shallots, lemon juice, lemon peel, vinegar, mustard, sugar, salt and pepper in a blender on low speed, and then slowly add the oil in a slow stream, blending until an emulsion forms. Stop blending once all the oil has been added. Taste and adjust the seasoning if needed.

*Makes about 1 $^1/_4$ cup.*


# classic white sauce

2 tablespoons butter
2 tablespoons flour
1$^1/_4$ cups milk, heated
$^1/_2$ teaspoon salt
$^1/_2$ teaspoon black pepper

Melt the butter in a heavy saucepan over medium heat. Stir in the flour and cook, stirring constantly, until the paste cooks and bubbles a bit, about 2 minutes (be careful not to let it brown). Add the hot milk, continuing to stir as the sauce thickens. Bring the sauce to a boil. Add the salt and pepper; lower the heat, and cook, stirring for 2 to 3 minutes more. Remove from the heat.

*Makes about 1 $^1/_2$ cups.*

# Butters for Crab Dipping
*These butters also make wonderful basting sauces when grilling crab.*

## orange basil butter

20 fresh basil leaves, chopped
2 tablespoons fresh orange juice
1 stick butter
salt and freshly ground white pepper
2 tablespoons olive oil

In a saucepan, combined the freshly chopped basil leaves with the butter. Over very low heat, melt the butter without letting it reach a simmer. Add oil, salt and pepper. Stir constantly to keep the butter thick and creamy. Remove from heat. Serve immediately or keep warm until ready to serve.

## chili jalapeño butter

1 tablespoon vegetable oil
1 jalapeño, ribbed, seeded, finely chopped
1 teaspoon dark chili powder
1 stick butter
juice of one-half lime

Sauté the jalapeño in the vegetable oil in a small pan over medium heat for 3-4 minutes. Add the chili powder and cook for one more minute. Add the butter and the lime juice. Remove from heat. Serve immediately or keep warm until ready to serve.

# citrus butter

1 stick butter
1 tablespoon grated lemon rind
1 tablespoon grated orange rind

Melt butter in a small saucepan. Add remaining ingredients. Heat gently 2-3 minutes. Serve immediately or keep warm until ready to serve.

# drawn butter

$^1/_2$ lb. unsalted butter

Place the butter in a small saucepan and bring to a boil over medium-high heat. Boil for 1 minute. Set the saucepan aside and let the butter settle, undisturbed. The milk solids will come to the top and the watery whey will collect on the bottom. Skim off the milk solids with a spoon and pour the drawn butter into a serving bowl or several small ramekins, taking care not to include the watery liquid in the bottom of the pan. Serve.

# garlic black pepper butter

2 cloves garlic, crushed
1 teaspoon vegetable oil
1 teaspoon fresh black pepper, cracked
1 stick butter

In a small pan over medium heat, sauté the garlic and oil for 3-4 minutes or until the garlic is soft and golden brown. Add the black pepper. Reduce heat to low. Add the butter and cook until melted. Serve immediately or keep warm until ready to serve.

# lemon anchovy butter

1 stick butter
2 teaspoons anchovy paste
1 teaspoon grated lemon rind
1 teaspoon fresh lemon juice

Melt butter in a small saucepan. Add remaining ingredients. Heat gently 2-3 minutes. Serve immediately or keep warm until ready to serve.

# lemon chervil butter

1 stick butter
4 tablespoons fresh lemon juice
8 sprigs chervil, leaves only, chopped (or substitute parsley)
1 teaspoon Old Bay Seasoning

In a small saucepan, melt butter over low heat.  Add lemon juice, chervil and Old Bay Seasoning.  Serve immediately or keep warm until ready to serve.

# lemon chive butter

I stick butter
2 tablespoons snipped fresh chives
1 teaspoon finely shredded lemon peel

In a small saucepan, melt butter. Remove from heat. Stir in chives and lemon peel. Serve immediately or keep warm until ready to serve.

## lemon pepper butter

1 stick butter
2 teaspoons pepper
1 teaspoon grated lemon rind
2 teaspoons fresh lemon juice

Melt butter in a small saucepan. Add remaining ingredients. Heat gently 2-3 minutes. Serve immediately or keep warm until ready to serve.

## lime cilantro butter

1 clove garlic, crushed
1 tablespoon vegetable oil
2 tablespoon chili pepper, finely chopped
$1/2$ teaspoon lime zest
juice of one lime
1 stick of butter

Sauté the garlic and oil in a small pan over medium heat for 3-4 minutes, or until the garlic is soft and golden brown. Add the chili pepper, lime juice and butter, cooking only until the butter is melted. Add the lime zest. Remove from heat. Serve immediately or keep warm until ready to serve.

## spicy herbed butter

1 lb unsalted butter at room temperature
3 cloves garlic, coarsely chopped
1 red jalapeño, seeds and white membranes removed, chopped coarsely
$^1/_4$ cup coarsely chopped Italian parsley leaves
1 lemon, juiced
3 tablespoons chopped chives
salt and freshly ground black pepper

Melt butter in a small saucepan. Add remaining ingredients. Heat gently 2-3 minutes.
Serve immediately or keep warm until ready to serve.

## tarragon butter

1 stick of butter
2 tablespoons chopped fresh tarragon
2 teaspoons crushed peppercorns
$^1/_2$ teaspoon salt
dash of hot sauce

Melt butter in a small saucepan. Add remaining ingredients. Heat gently 2-3 minutes.
Serve immediately or keep warm until ready to serve.

crab culture

# CRAB CULTURE

✤

*catching crab*
*crab catching methods and equipment*
*handling your catch*
*crabbing adventures*
*crabbing classes and clinics*
*crabbing vacations*
*crab festivals*

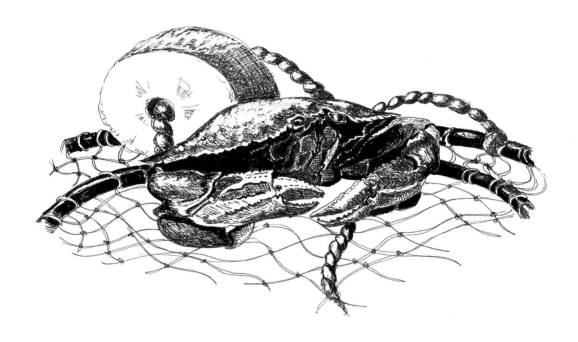

What could be more fun than catching your dinner? In fact, catching crab can be a fun and enjoyable experience for the whole family. I look forward to crab season each year. The excitement of hoisting up a pot full of crab is nothing short of thrilling. It actually requires very little equipment or skill, is relatively inexpensive, and is something everyone can do.

### Where to Catch Crab

Crab may be caught in shallow water, from boats, docks and piers. If you are new to crabbing and will be crabbing in an unfamiliar area, make a visit to the local marina or bait shops nearby, where they can fill you in on the local crabbing, which may include advice on the best places to crab. If you don't live close to an area where you can partake in this enjoyable endeavor, check crabbing adventures.

### Licenses and Registration

It's important to find out about the local regulations on crabbing, and whether a license is required or not. Local bait shops and sports stores will not only sell you bait and equipment, but also sell crabbing licenses and offer information about the area's rules on crabbing. See the appendix for a list of the various state agencies that publish booklets and maintain Web sites about local regulations. You'll find out that not all places require a license; in fact, most do not. And some places, for example, only allow people to keep crab of a certain size. So, remember, once you've caught your crab, measure them and make sure they are legal. A special crab ruler will help you do that.

### Crab Bait

Unless you're crabbing with a net, you'll need crab bait. If you'll be using a hand line, chicken necks work best. If you're baiting a trap or pot, there are several options: chicken parts, fish carcasses (especially salmon and fish heads) and clams have all worked well for us. Contrary to popular belief, crabs are not scavengers. They prefer fresh and live food, such as clams, mussels, shrimp and small fish. Crabs also eat vegetation, such as eel grass, sea lettuce and many other plants.

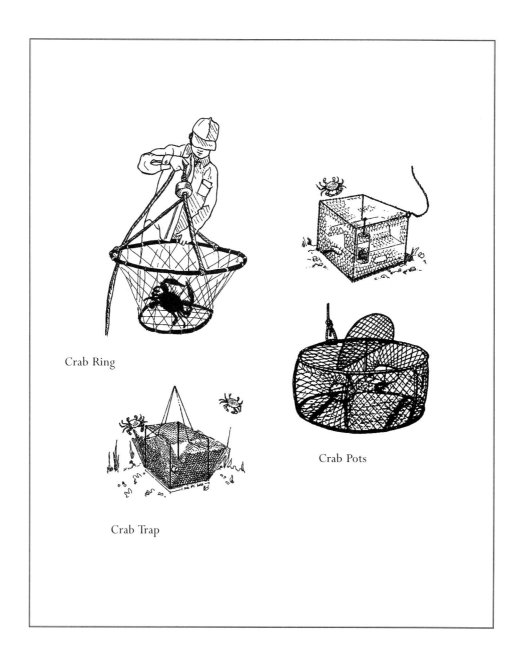

Crab Ring

Crab Pots

Crab Trap

# CRAB CATCHING METHODS AND EQUIPMENT

### Hand Line (or Bait Line) Crabbing

For this type of crabbing method, all that's needed is a long piece of string or fishing line, a chicken neck and a long-handed net, to scoop up the crab. This is often very successful and even young children can do this. First, tie a chicken neck to a line (string or fishing line that is long enough to reach the sea floor) and slowly lower it into the water. Then, watch the string closely. Once you see the line moving away or becoming taut, then the crab has the bait. Pull up the string in a slow, steady motion. As the crab comes into your vision in the water, very carefully slip the net under the crab and scoop him up. What could be easier?

### Crabbing with a Net

This method involves wading through shallow water at low tide. When you spot a crab, scoop up the crab from behind, and net it. This technique requires a bit more skill and practice than dropping a crab line, crab trap or crab pot. Netting can also be accomplished from a boat.

### Crabbing with a Crab Ring

A crab ring is also called a ring net. Perhaps the simplest and cheapest of all crab traps, the crab ring can be used from docks, piers and boats. It consists of two rings, each of a different diameter, connected by netting. The larger ring is open, while the smaller ring has netting secured across it. First, anchor the bait to the smaller ring's mesh. Then, lower the crab ring so that the rings lay flat on the sea floor, giving a crab easy access to the bait. Once a crab approaches and starts to feed on the bait, pull the trap straight up and fast. When the trap is pulled, the sides extend, turning the trap into a basket in which the crab is caught. A crab ring should be checked every 15 to 30 minutes.

### Crab Pots (or Crab Traps)

Crab pots, also called crab traps, come in various forms: round, square, fixed and collapsible. They have the advantage that they can be left unattended for long periods of time—in fact, they can be left to "soak" for several hours or overnight. A crab pot allows the crab to get in, but not get out. They can be used on a dock or from a boat, and is generally set in water about 20 to 150 feet deep. They have with a length of rope attached to it, and a buoy (or float) attached to the end of the rope. First, place the crab pot into the water and lower it straight down until you feel the pot touch the sea floor. It's important to do this, so you can be sure that the pot lands right-side up, and actually touches the bottom. This is why you never toss a crab pot into the water—you won't know what side up your pot will land and you can't be sure that the crab pot has reached the bottom. If the water's deeper than your line, you'll sadly watch your pot disappear as it sinks into the water . After allowing a crab pot to sit for a while, hoist it up with a quick and steady motion, pulling it straight up. When the pot feels heavy, that's a good sign that you've caught some crab (the exception to this is if the crab's mortal enemy, the starfish, has climbed aboard).

## HANDLING YOUR CATCH

You may want to wear thick gloves to help you safely handle these feisty little devils. Always approach from the rear when you are about to pick up a crab. Simply reach down and grab one or both hind legs.

After a few times, you will find this very easy and natural. If you should find yourself with a crab scurrying on the ground, don't worry. Simply press lightly on the top shell with a shoe, stick, or other hard item, being careful not to use too much pressure (or the shell will crack).

Should a crab get a hold of your finger, it is usually best not to try to pull it off. Instead, try letting it hang; many times the crab will release on its own and drop. If that doesn't work, use your free hand to immobilize the other claw while slowly bending the offending claw backward until the crab lets go.

You'll need a container to store your catch: coolers, buckets and baskets all work well. Whatever you use, make sure it has a lid (you don't want them escaping) and is ventilated. Keep your catch out of the sun, and never submerge crab in water, because they'll quickly use up the oxygen and drown. Instead, soak a cloth or paper in salt water and cover the crab with it. Although crab are able to live for days out of water, cooking them within a day is best.

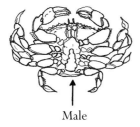

Male

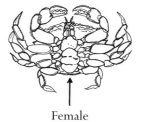

Female

CRABBING ADVENTURES

**Adventure Cruises, Inc.**
Suite G, Harbourside III
Shelter Cove Harbour
Hilton Head Island, South Carolina 29928
843-785-4558
www.hiltonheadisland.com
*Join the crabby crew on a sport crabbing adventure. The boat motors out to the calm waters of Broad Creek and anchors up next to the salt marsh, where everyone fishes for the sly and cunning blue crab. It's all catch and release, just for fun, but the crabby crew keeps score: Whoever catches the most, wins the world famous Crabber J T-shirt. The program runs April through October.*

**Jade Lady Charters**
22121 Beaven Dr.
Denton, Maryland 21629
410-364-9057
www.chesapeakebay-fishing.com
*A day of crabbing in Chesapeake Bay begins at 6:00 AM, with all the bait and the equipment supplied by the captain. In the afternoon, sit back and enjoy your freshly caught steamed crabs and the surrounding natural beauty.*

**Five Star Charters**
Port of Gold Beach
Gold Beach, Oregon 97444
888-301-6480
www.goldbeachadventures.com
*Bring your shellfish license and big appetites for an afternoon of crabbing. These trips can yield up to 12 crab per person. The crew cleans and cooks your catch, too. Trips operate December through August.*

**Florida Keys Adventures**
End of 35th Street on the Gulf
Marathon, Florida 33050
866-743-4353
www.keysfisheries.com
*Join the crew for a day aboard a commercial stone crab or lobster boat. You will spend 3 to 3½ hours with a commercial fisherman, while your boat pulls lobster or stone-crab traps and you remove the catch. When you return to the docks, your catch can be prepared at the dockside restaurant, or you can have your catch packed and shipped. Each group can expect to receive 8 pounds of either lobster or stone crab, depending on the season.*

**All Aboard Adventures with Captain Tim**
Noyo Harbor
Fort Bragg, California 95437
707-964-1881
www.allaboardadventures.com
*Spend a day in Noyo Harbor, where you will bait crab pots, drop them in the ocean, and pick up them full of crab on the way back to shore. Enjoy your day's catch during a shoreside picnic meal. When rock cod and salmon are in season, you can go on a longer "combo trip," where you can spend some time fishing before harvesting the crab.*

**Crab Boat Charters**
PO Box 816
Manteo, North Carolina 27954
252-255-CRAB (2722)
www.outerbankscruises.com
*Experience life as a commercial fisherman working the calm island waters of The Outer Banks. Learn firsthand about commercial fishing and crabbing from a 10th-generation island native, as Captain Kevin Wescott shares part of his world with you. Sort the catch from the net and keep the crabs, fish and shrimp in season.*

**Mischief II Charters with Captain Joe Schwartz**
21710 Deep Harbor Farm Road
Sherwood, Maryland 21665
410-886-2085
www.toad.net/~mischief2/
*Join Captain Joe Schwartz aboard Mischief II for some of the best fishing and crabbing that Maryland's Chesapeake Bay has to offer. Full-day, half-day, and combination charters are available for parties up to 6. The trips leave from Sherwood, Maryland (located between St. Michaels and Tilghman Island). Also, off-shore fishing trips are available, leaving from Ocean City, Maryland, from mid-August through mid-September.*

**Cattus Island Park Crabbing Tour**
Ocean County Department of Parks and Recreation
1198 Bandon Road
Toms River, New Jersey 08753
877-OC PARKS
www.co.ocean.nj.us/Parks/default.htm
*The staff of Cattus Island Park are proud to present the best Barnegat Bay has to offer. Cattus Island Park's pontoon boat, the Betty 'C', will transport participants to crabbing and fishing locations in Mosquito Cove. Those wishing to fish should bring poles and bait. Those wishing to crab should bring traps and bait; or lines, bait and nets. While they don't guarantee a great catch, they do guarantee a great time. And best of all, it's free! Pre-registration is required. Children need to be at least four years old to participate.*

**Port of Alsea**
365 A Port Street
Waldport, Oregon 97394
541-563-3872
www.portofalsea.com
*Located on the waterfront, just upriver from the mouth of Alsea Bay, Alsea Port's public facilities include Public docks for crabbing, a boat launch ramp, boat moorage, great beach access and a picnic area. An accessible viewing platform and crabbing float give visitors a close-up look at marine life while crabbing. Crab rings, bait, boat rentals and fishing tackle are available nearby.*

**Fort Point Pier**
Presidio
San Francisco, California 94129
415-556-1693
www.nps.gov/fopo
*Twice a month from March through October, Golden Gate National Recreation Area offers families a chance to crab from Fort Point Pier in the Presidio. Rangers supply the crabbing nets and insights on how to snag these creatures. Children ages 3 and up may participate. On selected Saturday's, two-hour-long crabbing classes are held. The fee is $1.50, which goes toward bait. Call for more information and reservations.*

**Pea Island National Wildlife Refuge**
P.O. Box 1969
Manteo, NC 27954
252-987-2394
http://peaisland.fws.gov
*Billed as a family event, the annual Fishing and Crabbing Rodeo is one of the most anticipated events on the Outer Banks of North Carolina. For one day in June, North Pond is open to the public for crabbing and fishing. All participants will need to bring their own crabbing gear.*

**Sandy Point State Park**
1100 East College Parkway
Annapolis, Maryland 21401
888-432-2267
www.toad.net/~mischief2
*This 786-acre park on the Chesapeake Bay has a crabbing and fishing pier, located at the south end of the boat launch ramps. The marina store sells crabbing supplies. The park's beaches and picnic areas provide unparalleled views of the Bay.*

## CRABBING CLINICS AND CLASSES

**Heron Park Nature Center**
4000 Seaforest Drive
Kiawah Island, South Carolina 29455
843-768-6001
*Catch crab the old-fashioned way, with a line and chicken neck. Venture by boat to an excellent crabbing spot. And then return to the beach for a crab boil, where you'll enjoy your catch. The crabbing clinic runs from May through October. Call for reservations.*

**Barrier Island Environmental Education Program**
2810 Seabrook Island Road
Johns Island, South Carolina 29455
843-768- 0429
www.stchristopher.org
*The "Claws" class teaches students how to catch crab using baited crab lines, and how to cook and 'pick' a crab for its meat. Discussions cover topics such as commercial crabbing, and the importance of crabbing to Native Americans. The classes are offered late March through mid-November.*

**'Becoming an Outdoors Woman' (BOW) Program**
The Oregon Department of Fish and Wildlife
3406 Cherry Avenue NE
Salem, Oregon 97303
503-947-6000
www.dfw.state.or.us
*This award-winning program offers hands-on crabbing classes. Although the program is largely designed for and taught by women, men may also attend. Call for dates and to make reservations.*

## CRABBING VACATIONS

**Cherrystone Family Camping Resort**
P.O. Box 545
Cheriton, Virginia 23316
757-331-3063
www.cherrystoneva.com
*Situated on 300 acres of waterfront on the beautiful Chesapeake Bay, Cherrystone offers log cabins, deluxe cottages, and camp sites for trailers and tents. Four piers are well-situated for both crabbing and fishing. From June through September, an abundance of crab can be caught from the piers. Oysters and clams may be gathered using rakes. The bait-and-tackle shop carries everything you'll need for crabbing. Crab races for kids are held every week.*

**Ewell Tide Bed & Breakfast**
Smith Island
Ewell, Maryland 21824
888-699-2141
www.smithisland.net
*The Ewell Tide is a bed and breakfast inn, located on Smith Island in the heart of the Chesapeake Bay. The folks at Ewell's Tide will happily show you how to throw over a crabbing line from the Smith Island Marina dock and catch blue crab from the shallows.*

**Embarcadero Resort Hotel and Marina**
1000 S.E. Bay Boulevard
Newport, Oregon 97365
800-547-4779
www.embarcadero-resort.com
*This hotel is located in a beautiful setting on the Oregon Coast. Guests can enjoy crabbing from the resort's private crab dock, and cook their catch in the crab cooker on the beach. The general store offers crabbing equipment and boats for rent, and bait and licenses for sale. Crabbing is open year-round, and classes are available each week.*

**Groveland Cottage - Crabbing Adventure**
4861 Sequim-Dungeness Way
Sequim, Washington 98382
800-879-8859
*You'll catch crab the way many locals do, wading through the water with hip or chest waders, scooping up the crab with special pitchforks, and then depositing them into a bucket. Groveland Cottage offers a crabbing adventure package, which includes two nights lodging, two breakfasts, the crabbing adventure, and one crab dinner for two. It also includes the gear (hip or chest waders, pitch forks, buckets, lanterns, etc. Not included is a crabbing license. An out-of-state license for 3 days is $6.00 (in-state is $5.00 per year).*

# CRAB FESTIVALS

## California

### *San Francisco's Annual Crab Festival – San Francisco*
January 31 to February 28.
San Francisco honors the legendary Dungeness crab with a month of feasting and celebration. Evens in the annual celebration include "Challenge of Masters", "Walk About the Wharf" and "Crab and Wine Marketplace". Highlights include gourmet crab specialties, fresh seafood and wine tasting, chef demonstrations, live music, performances, arts and crafts, and a children's crab-themed recreation area. Events are held at Fisherman's Wharf, Union Square and North Beach.
Information: www.sfvisitor.org or (415) 391-2000

### *Mendocino Crab and Wine Days – Mendocino*
With its scenic oceanfront and quaint downtown, Mendocino County plays host to the annual "Wine and Crab Days". Cooking demonstrations and wine- and appetizer-tasting are combined with the popular Crab Cake Cook-off and Best Mendocino Crab Wine Competition. As part of the special events, charter boats will take crab lovers on cruises to learn about crabbing, or to do some serious all-day fishing and crabbing. This is a celebration of the region's crab and wine industries where lots of food and fun is the catch of the day. Participating restaurants offer daily crab specials and host winemaker dinners are featured throughout the festival
Information: www.goMendo.com or 866-goMendo (866) 466-3636)

## Florida

### *Blue Crab Festival – Panacea*
1st weekend in May.
For over thirty years, the Annual Panacea Blue Crab Festival is one of the largest such festivals on Florida's northern Gulf Coast. The festivities begin with a morning parade on the Coastal Highway 98. Demonstrations and contests are held, including crab picking, crab trap pulling and a mullet toss, with one of the largest fireworks display in the region for a concluding event.
Information: info@bluecrabfest.com or call (850) 984-CRAB (2722)

### *Blue Crab Festival – Palatka*
Always Memorial Day weekend.
Who would have thought that a little crustacean could cause all this hoopla? With crabs boiling, music bopping and libations flowing, Palatka's Blue Crab Festival has established itself as a bona

fide North Florida phenomenon. Some 100,000 visitors celebrate this 4-day festival on the riverfront, which feature arts and crafts, rides, entertainment and lots of food.
Information: www.bluecrabfestival.com. or call (386) 325 – 4406

*Annual Stone Crab, Seafood & Wine Festival – Longboat Key*
October 30 – November 2.
For each of the past fifteen years, The Colony on Longboat key has celebrated the beginning of Stone Crab season by inviting this nation's leading chefs and vintners to join its guests for a long weekend of fabulous food and wine in a beautiful setting at the edge of the water, blue-green waters of the Gulf of Mexico.
Information: (941) 383-6464, Ext. 2854

## Louisiana

*Bayou Lacombe Crab Festival – Lacombe*
Last week in June.
A scenic one-hour drive from New Orleans, the Bayou Lacombe Crab Festival takes place at John Davis Park, a pretty setting canopied by huge live oak trees. Each year, about 2,000 blue crabs, Louisiana's most prominent crab type, are boiled at the festival. At one end of the park are carnival rides, and at the other end, some 50+ craft booths are set up. There are also activities for the kiddies and live music throughout the weekend.
Information:  www.lacombecrabfestival.com  or call (985) 892-0520 or (800) 634-9443

## Maryland

*National Hard Crab Derby & Fair - Crisfield*
Always Labor Day weekend.
Three days of exciting events including the famous Crab Derby itself. Crabs from as far away as Hawaii have competed in the run for the Governor's Cup. Colorful parades, beauty pageants, boat races, arts and craft exhibits, crab picking contest, swim meet, a carnival, games and lots of great food contribute to this event.
Information:  www.crisfieldchamber.com or call Crisfield Area Chamber of Commerce,
P.O.Box 292, Crisfield, MD 21817   (800) 782-3913

*Crab Days at Chesapeake Bay Maritime Museum – St. Michaels*
Last weekend in July - Saturday & Sunday - 10am - 5 pm
Celebrate the Maryland blue crab!  Enjoy live music, boat rides and cooking demonstrations. Indulge in steamed crabs, crab cake, crab soup and more. Crab Days has a double focus – food and (educational) fun.  Crabbing demonstrations will include trot lining, chicken necking, crab pot making and, for newcomers to the Chesapeake Bay area, crab picking. Try your hand at these tasks. A special Kids town area provides plenty of activities for children including the crab toss, the touch tank, face painting, a scavenger hunt and the ever-popular crab races.

## Oregon

*The Astoria-Warrenton Crab & Seafood Festival*
Last full weekend in April
With a crab fest, Oregon wines and food and crafts booths, this is one of the top festivals in Oregon, held at the Clatsop County Fairgrounds. It is open to all ages with entertainment for all including a petting zoo and crab races. Together with crab, seafood and a wide assortment of foods, one can sample wine from 36 Oregon wineries. Held at Hammond Mooring Basin on the Columbia River, festivities include arts and crafts vendors, children's activities and continuous live music.
Information: Astoria-Warrenton Chamber of Commerce at (800) 875-6807 or (503) 325-6311
www.oldoregon.com

*Cruzin' for Crab, Crab Festival & Chowder Tasting – Waldport*
Enjoy Dungeness crab dinners, chowder tasting, and fun for all ages. Catch your own crab off the dock, or rent a boat for the day. Tour the specialty cars on display. Stop by the beer garden. Dance to the music; wander through craft and display booths.
Information: (541) 563-5200

## South Carolina

*Annual Little River Blue Crab Festival – Little River*
May 15-16.
Held on the Waterfront in historic Little River, the Blue Crab Festival is Little River's main claim to fame, and the little village does not hold back. The Blue Crab Festival is a combination of arts, crafts and, of course, food – namely crab.  After eating, you can dance the day away with live entertainment ranging from jazz to bluegrass to gospel.
Information: (843) 385-3180 or info@bluecrabftestival.org

**Washington**

*Dungeness Crab and Seafood Festival – Sequim*
2nd weekend in October
The Dungeness Crab & Seafood Festival celebrates the foods and traditions of the Olympic Peninsula with its primary focus on the world-famous Dungeness crab and the communities that are sustained by the natural environment of the Olympic Peninsula.  The Festival occurs annually during the second weekend of October, coinciding with the beginning of crab season.  Festival activities take place in downtown Port Angeles on the city pier
Information: Denise Price (360) 457-6110 or info@crabfestival.org

*Westport Crab Festival*
3rd weekend in May.
Highlights include crab races, a crab derby and a crab feed along with a family dance. The two-day festival includes a crab feed, crab lore and demonstrations.
Information: (800) 345-6223

sources & resources

# SOURCES & RESOURCES

❧

*mail order crab*

*sources*

*online resources*

*crabbing supplies and gear*

*appendix: crabbing regulations by state*

## MAIL ORDER CRAB

A craving for crab can strike at any time. I've taken great care in compiling a list of established, reputable businesses that will supply you with great crab. If ordering live crab, it's best to arrange for the crab to arrive the day you plan to cook it.

### Annapolis Seafood Market—Annapolis, MD

This market has been in business for over 20 years. Blue crab is available live or steamed, and is sold by the dozen. Soft-shell crab is available fresh, and is sold individually. Fresh and pasteurized crabmeat is available by the pound. Call 410-263-7787 or go to annapolisseafoodmarket.com.

### Best Stone Crabs—Everglades City, FL

They specialize in stone crab, caught with their own fleet of boats and cooked upon arrival at their dockside facility. Medium, large, jumbo and colossal claws are offered. Fresh stone crab is available October 15th to May 15th. Frozen stone crab may be purchased in the other months. All orders are packed with iced gel packs in reusable Styrofoam® containers and shipped overnight via FedEx®.

### Cap'n Zach's—McKinleyville, CA

Cap'n Zach's offers Dungeness crab right off the boat. Crab can be shipped live or fresh cooked. Fresh crabmeat is also available. They are open from December 1st through Labor Day and are closed on Mondays. Call 707-839-9059 or go to  www.crabfeed.com.

### City Fish—Pike Place Market, Seattle, WA

Established in 1917, City Fish is the longest-running fish market at Pike Place Market. City Fish offers whole cooked Dungeness crab, Alaskan king crab and fresh crabmeat. City fish also sells a variety of live clams and mussels. They offer overnight shipping to anywhere in the US. Call 800-334-2669 or go to www.cityfish.com.

### Lighthouse Deli and Fish Company—South Beach, OR

The Lighthouse buys live crab directly from fishermen and cook them in their 'crab cooker' located in the front of the store. Dungeness crab can be purchased whole cooked and fresh crabmeat is available by the pound. Both are shipped overnight.
Call 866-816-7716 or go to www.lighthousedeli.com.

**Mutual Fish Co—Seattle, WA**

The Mutual Fish Company is a retail-wholesale seafood market, owned and operated by three generations of the Yoshimura family since 1947. My sister-in law and her husband are longtime customers. Dungeness crab is available whole, live or cooked; crab legs are available fresh or frozen; and crabmeat can be had fresh or frozen. Alaskan king crab legs are available fresh once or twice a year. Call 206-322-4368 or go to www.mutualfish.com.

**The Crab Place—Crisfield, MD**

Blue crab can be ordered steamed or live. Live soft-shell crab is also offered. Frozen king crab and snow crab legs are sold by the pound. Fresh and pasteurized crabmeat is sold by the pound. A great bonus of ordering with The Crab Place is that they ship extra crab with every order, to compensate for any that may perish in transit. Call 877-EAT-CRAB or go to www.crabplace.com.

**W. H. Harris Seafood—Grasonville, MD**

This has been a family-owned and operated business for over 50 years. Chesapeake Bay blue crab is available fresh in season, and frozen during the winter months. Crab can be ordered live or steamed, and packed in or 1 or 2-bushels. Fresh crabmeat is also available and is sold by the pound. Orders are processed Monday through Thursday. Orders are shipped overnight via FedEx® or UPS®. Call 410-827-8104 or go to www.harriscrabhouse.com.

## Cajun Grocer

116 Alley 3
Lafayette, Louisiana 70506
888-CRAWFISH
www.cajungrocer.com
CajunGrocer.com is the largest online seller of genuine Louisiana foods. Visitors will find more than 400 top-brand products to choose from, including Zatarain's and Tony Chachere's Creole Seasonings, filé powder and crawfish. Order through the Web site or by calling the toll-free number, 24 hours a day, seven days a week.

## Maryland Delivered

2200 Sykesville Rd. (Rt. 32)
Westminster, MD 21157
1-888-284-8565
www.marylanddelivered.com
Source for Old Bay and J.O.Seasonings. J.O. Seasoning, although lesser known, is used almost exclusively in the crab houses of Maryland .Order through the Web site,  toll-free number or the retail location.

## Crate and Barrel

Retail locations throughout U.S.
800-967-6696
www.crateandbarrel.com
Butter warmers, crab forks, shell buckets. Lots of fun seafood oriented items such as serving platters, napkins and glasses for your crab feast. Most of these items are seasonal so you'll find them in the summer mail-order catalog and in the store seasonally.

## Sur La Table

84 Pine Street
Seattle, WA  98101
www.surlatable.com
1-800-243-0852
A Cook's paradise since 1972. There are over 44 Sur La Table stores in the United States.  This is a store I can spend hours in and often do. They carry a large array of butter warmers, crab forks and picks, shellfish cracker sets, shellfish pots, bibs, and many shellfish themed items. If you can't make it to one of their stores, they've got a terrific Web site and catalog that comes out several times a year.

**The Spanish Table**
Various Locations
510-548-1383
505-986-0243
www.spanishtable.com
The Spanish Table carries an extensive selection of Spanish and Portuguese food and cookware, including a staggering array of paella pans. Order through the Web site or visit one of their stores.

**The Crab Cracker**
Crabcracker.net
The design simplicity of "The Crab Cracker" makes cracking crab fun and easy. In a fraction of the time it takes utilizing a traditional hand-held device the "Crab Cracker" produces crabmeat free from embedded shell fragments and without the mess associated with hand-held crackers. Available on-line or at various retail stores.

**Pacific Rim Gourmet**
4905 Morena Boulevard, Suite 1313
San Diego, CA 92117
1-800-910-WOKS
www.pacificrim-gourmet.com
 Great on-line source for full range of Asian ingredients and kitchen ware.
Order through the Web site or toll-free number.

**McFadden Farm**
16000 Powerhouse Rd.
Potter Valley, California 95469
800-544-8230
www.mcfaddenfarm.com
McFadden Farm grows and sells a wide variety of organic herbs and herb blends. I use their garlic powder, which is superior to any other I've used. My favorite blends are the Mexican Blend and Beef Herbs. (which I use in a variety of dishes)

ONLINE RESOURCES

**The Blue Crab Archives**

www.blue-crab.org

This Web site has everything you'd like to know about the Atlantic blue crab. Learn about its history, and where and how it lives, eats and reproduces; participate in a discussion forum; read about the latest blue crab news; and lots more.

**Blue Crab Home Page**

www.blue-crab.net

This Web site serves as a great overview of blue crab biology, ecology, regulations and fishery, and has links to many other related Web sites.

**Dungeness Web Site**

www.dungeness.com

Learn all about the Dungeness crab and the town from which the shell fish derived its name, including harvesting methods, crabbing regulations and much more.

**Oregon Dungeness Crab Commission**

www.//uci.net/~dcrab/

This Web site offers information about Oregon State's crabbing industry, crab nutritional information, crab biology and more.

**Seafood Choices Alliance**

www.seafoodchoices.org

Bringing ocean conservation to the table: Seafood Choices Alliance provides seafood purveyors, such as chefs and retailers, with the information they need to meet both an economic and environmental bottom line.

**Seafood Watch**

www.mbayaq.org/cr/seafoodwatch.asp

A program of Monterey Bay Aquarium designed to raise consumer awareness about the importance of buying seafood from sustainable sources. They recommend which seafood to buy or avoid, helping consumers to become advocates for environmentally friendly seafood

**Crabbing on the Oregon Coast**

http://www.scod.com/cities/crabs/crabbing.html

All you need to know about crabbing on the Oregon coast, including regulations, where to crab, what kind of equipment to use, how to use them and more.

## CRABBING SUPPLIES AND GEAR

**McKay Shrimp and Crab Gear**
32 Easy Street
Brinnon, Washington  98320
360-796-4555
www.mckayshrimpandcrabgear.com
In business since the mid 1970s, this is where my husband and I purchase our crab pots. We use their "No Escape" crab pot. McKay's has an online catalog, accepts Visa or Master Card, and will ship via USPS, truck freight lines, or UPS. All orders are shipped within 24 hours, and are guaranteed to be of the finest quality available in today's market place.

**Blue Ocean Tackle**
P.O. Box 3042
Rancho Cucamonga, California 91729
www.blueoceantackle.com
Extensive on-line source for crabbing supplies. Site also has information on crabbing.

**Bill's Sport Shop**
1566 Highway One
Lewes, Delaware 19958
302-645-7654
www.billssportshop.com
Here's an online catalog with everything you need for crabbing, including large steamers for cooking your catch.

# APPENDIX:

Crabbing Regulations by State

Contact one of the following agencies for information about the regulations governing the taking of crabs in the state where you will be enjoying your crabbing adventure:

Alabama Department of Conservation and Natural Resources
Game and Fish Division
64 North Union Street
Montgomery, Alabama 36130
334-242-3465 or 334-220-3465
www.dcnr.state.al.us/agfd


Alaska Department of Fish and Game
P.O. Box 2256
Juneau, Alaska 99802-5526
907-465-4100
www.adfg.state.ak.us

California Department of Fish and Game
1416 9th Street, Room 1320
Sacramento, California 95814
916-653-1856
www.dfg.ca.gov

State of Connecticut
Department of Environmental Protection
79 Elm Street
Hartford, Connecticut 06106-5127
860-424-3000
www.dep.state.ct.us

Delaware Division of Fish & Wildlife
89 Kings Highway
Dover, Delaware 19901
302-739-5297
www.dnrec.state.de.us/dnrec2000

Florida Division of Marine Resources
Department of Environmental Protection
3900 Commonwealth Boulevard, Room 843
Tallahassee, Florida 32303
850-488-6058
www.floridaconservation.org

Florida Fish and Wildlife Conservation Commission
620 South Meridian Street
Tallahassee, Florida 32399-1600
www.floridaconservation.org

Georgia Department of Natural Resources
Law Enforcement
Coastal Resources Division
One Conservation Way
Brunswick, Georgia 311523
912-264-7237
www.georgiawildlife.dnr.state.ga.us/

State of Hawaii
Department of Land and Natural Resources
Division of Aquatic Resources
1151 Punchbowl Street, Room 330
Honolulu, Hawaii 96813
808-587-0100
www.hawaii.gov/dlnr/dar/regbk/index.html

Louisiana Department of Wildlife and Fisheries
Enforcement Division
P.O. Box 98000
Baton Rouge, Louisiana 70898-9000
504-765-24469
www.wlf.state.la.us/apps/netgear/page1.asp

Maine Department of Marine Resources
Hallowell B 21 State House Station
Augusta, Maine 04333-0021
207-624-6550
www.state.me.us/dmr

Maryland Department of Natural Resources
580 Taylor Avenue
Tawes State Office Building
Annapolis, Maryland 21401
410-260-8250
www.dnr.state.md.us

Massachusetts Department of Fisheries, Wildlife and Environmental Law Enforcement
Division of Marine Fisheries
Leverett Saltonstall Building, Government Center
100 Cambridge Street, Room 1901
Boston, Massachusetts 02202
617-727-3193
www.mass.gov/dfwele/dfw/dfw_toc.htm

New Hampshire Fish & Game Department
Law Enforcement Division
2 Hazen Drive
Concord, New Hampshire 03301-6500
603-271-3127
www.wildlife.state.nh.us

New Jersey Department of Environmental Protection
401 East State Street
7th Floor, East Wing
P.O. Box 402
Trenton, New Jersey 08625-0402
609-292-2885
www.state.nj.us/dep/fgw
www.nj.gov/dep/index.html

New York State Department of Environmental Conservation
Office of Natural Resources
Division of Fish, Wildlife, and Marine Resources
50 Wolf Road
Albany, New York 12233
518-457-5690
www.dec.state.ny.us/website/dfwmr

North Carolina Department of Environmental and Natural Resources
Division of Marine Fisheries
3441 Arendell Street
Morehead City, North Carolina 28557
252-726-7021
www.ncfisheries.net

Oregon Department of Fish and Wildlife
Fish Division
2501 Southwest 1st Avenue
Portland, Oregon 97207
503-872-5252
Shellfish regulations: 541-867- 4741
www.dfw.state.or.us

Rhode Island Division of Environmental Management
Division of Fish and Wildlife
4808 Tower Hill Road
Wakefield, Rhode Island 02879
401-222-3075 or 789-3094
www.state.ri.us

South Carolina Department of Natural Resources
Marine Resource Division
Office of Fisheries Management, Shellfish Management Program
217 Fort Johnson Road
Charleston, South Carolina 29412
843-953-9300
www.dnr.state.sc.us

Texas Parks and Wildlife Department
Coastal Fishing Division
4200 Smith School Road
Austin, Texas 78744
512-389-4800
www.tpwd.state.tx.us/fish/coastal.htm

Virginia Marine Resources Commission
P.O. Box 756
2600 Washington Avenue
Newport News, Virginia  23607-0756
757-247-2200
www.dgif.state.va.us/fishing

Virginia Department of Game and Inland Fisheries
4010 West Broad Street
Richmond, Virginia  23230
804-367-1000
http://www.dgif.state.va.us/
Washington Department of Fish and Wildlife
Natural Resources Building
1121 Washington Street S.E.
Olympia, Washington  98501
360-902-2200
www.wdfw.wa.gov/fish-sh.htm

# BIBLIOGRAPHY

Beard, James. *James Beard's Shellfish.* New York: Thames and Hudson, 1997.

Beard, James. *James Beard's New Fish Cookery.* Boston: Little, Brown, 1976.

Bittman, Mark. *Fish: The Complete Guide to Buying and Cooking.* New York: Hungry Minds, 1994.

Brannon, Nancy. *All About Crab, The Crab Lover's Guide to Dungeness.* Florence: Con Amore, 2000.

Brown, Helen Evans. *Helen Brown's West Coast Cookbook.* Boston: Little, Brown, 1952.

Davidson, Alan. *North Atlantic Seafood: A Comprehensive Guide.* New York: Viking. 1980.

Davidson, Alan. *The Oxford Companion to Food.* Oxford: University Press, 1999.

Day, Glen. *Crab Cookery Coast to Coast.* California: Crossing Press, 1982.

Duytt, Roberta Larson. *American Dietetic Association Complete Food and Nutrition Guide.* New Jersey: John Wiley & Sons, 2002.

Herbst, Sharon Tyler. *The New Food Lovers' Companion.* New York: Barron's, 2001.

Herbst, Sharon Tyler. *The New Food Lovers' Tiptionary.* New York: William Morrow, 2002.

Hillman, Howard. *The New Kitchen Science.* Boston: Houghton Mifflin Company, 2002.

Leon, Warren and De Wal, Caroline Smith. *Is Our Food Safe: A Consumer's Guide to Protecting Your Heart and the Environment.* California: Random House, 2002.

McGee, Harold. *On Food and Cooking.* New York: Scribner's, 1984.

MontagnJ, Prosper *The New Larousse Gastronomique.* New York: Crown,1997.

Oberrecht, Kenn. *Fish and Shellfish Care and Cookery.* New Jersey: Stoeger Publishing Company, 1997.

Orso, Mary Ethelyn. *The Crab Lover's Book.* Jackson: University Press of Mississippi, 1995.

Peterson, James. *Fish and Shellfish.* New York: William Morrow, 1996.

Prudhomme, Paul. *Paul Prudhomme's Louisiana Kitchen.* New York: Morrow, 1984.

Reaske, Christopher. *The Complet Crab and Lobster Book.* New Jersey: Burford Books. 1999

Roberts, Russel. *All About Blue Crab and How to Catch Them.* Grand Junction: Centennial, 1993

Rosso, Julie and Lukins, Sheila. *The New Basics.* New York: Workman, 1989.

Warner, William W. *Beautiful Swimmers.* Boston: Little, Brown & Co., 1994.

White, Charles. *How To Catch Crab.* Sidney, B.C.: Saltaile Publishing. 1975

*Jennifer Bellinger is a professional artist internationally*
*known for her wildlife, landscape and still life paintings.*

*Jennifer's paintings have won many awards in national juried*
*shows and her work is represented in public, corporate and private collections*
*in the USA, Canada, Europe, Australia and South Africa.*

*Jennifer lives in Ketchum, Idaho with her husband, Gary and son, Corey.*
*She and Gary lived in Ketchikan, Alaska in the 1970s and*
*enjoyed fishing and crabbing.*

*You may email Jennifer at: Jbellingerart@AOL.com*
*www.natureartist.com/jbellinger.htm*